Get Your War On

Get Your War On

The definitive account of the
War on Terror, 2001–2008

David Rees

Soft Skull Press   Brooklyn   2008

Library of Congress Cataloging-in-Publication Data

Rees, David, 1972–
  [Get your war on. Selections]
  Get your war on : the definitive account of the War on Terror, 2001–2008 / David Rees.
      p. cm.
  ISBN-13: 978-1-59376-213-1
  ISBN-10: 1-59376-213-5
  1. Comic books, strips, etc. 2. War on Terrorism, 2001—Comic books, strips, etc. I. Title.
  PN6728.G435R46 2008
  741.5'6973—dc22

                            2008029628

Cover design by David Rees
Interior design by David Janik
Printed in the United States of America

Comics marked with an asterisk have been modified or condensed since their initial publication.

Get Your War On is not licensed, sponsored, authorized, or endorsed by World Events Productions Ltd., which owns copyright and trademark rights in the "Voltron" character.

Soft Skull Press
An Imprint of Counterpoint LLC
2117 Fourth Street
Suite D
Berkeley, CA 94710

www.softskull.com
www.counterpointpress.com

Distributed by Publishers Group West

10 9 8 7 6 5 4 3 2 1

For Sarah, finally.

To avoid a quarrel is a setback for sin, for it is a hot temper that kindles quarrels.

A sinner sows trouble between friends and spreads scandal where before there was peace.

A fire is kept hot by stoking and a quarrel by persistence. A man's rage is in proportion to his strength, and his anger in proportion to his wealth.

A hasty argument kindles a fire, and a hasty quarrel leads to bloodshed.

Blow on a spark to make it glow, or spit on it to put it out; both results come from the one mouth.

—Ecclesiasticus (28:8-12)

INTRODUCTION by Matt Taibbi

Most artists have to worry about their legacies, but not David Rees. Even if he never moves a muscle for the rest of his life—and from what I understand, he is seriously considering this as a future career option—David Rees will have one tremendous accomplishment that he can always fall back on. And that is this: from September 11, 2001 through (according to my calculations) about the middle of 2004, David Rees was the only thing about America that was funny. He continued to be funny after that, and still is today, but for that one stretch, he was the *only* person in this country earning real laughs.

That's a nearly three-year period. I don't think any one person has ever held down that distinction for more than two or three straight months, at least not in modern times. Then again, there hasn't been a more starkly unfunny stretch of American history, perhaps, than the post-9/11 years when *Get Your War On* became famous.

If you're thinking the Great Depression had to be less funny, you couldn't be more wrong: in point of fact, the Depression was a time when America's artists showed great humility and civic instinct, trying to distract America from its problems with great literary comedies like *My Life and Hard Times* and movies like *Duck Soup* and *What, No Beer?*

After that? Well, even the darkest days of the Cold War produced comic masterpieces like *Catch-22* and *Dr. Strangelove,* proving that the staid, sexually repressed, racist America of the fifties and early sixties was still capable of laughing at its own bullshit.

The self-mocking instinct actually grew from there, and in fact was so entrenched by the late sixties that the would-be historically unfunny Nixon presidency was launched into history covered in comic barnacles, from R. Crumb's comics to the *Fear and Loathing* books to the film *M*A*S*H* to Richard Pryor, etc. It's probably not a coincidence that some of the funniest years in our history came when our international stature was at its lowest—in the late sixties and early seventies, when Chicago and Watts and Watergate and the appalling CIA hearings and the slog in Vietnam and our plummeting, gas-starved economy (sound familiar?) conspired to make America look, to the rest of the world, like a pathetic, schizoid joke.

From that point forward, though, things changed. For the next thirty years America undertook an unceasing reactionary effort to inoculate itself not only from laughter but from criticism of any sort. We spent twenty years or so trying to get over the bummer of our moral and military failure in Vietnam; our solution was a bogus "pride-restoring" war to defend Kuwait in the early nineties—a war fought to defend an ally with dubious humanitarian credentials, waged against an enemy that could not possibly fight back fairly. We rallied behind the president, speed-boat driving tool that he was, and cheerfully watched the victorious carnage on television, no longer caring that the military had complete control over what we did and didn't see from the war zone. So what if we didn't see casualties? Why interrupt the spectacle of combat with images of death and murder? The point was to bring the pride back—to feel good about ourselves again!

America by the late nineties was a preposterous caricature of a proud empire: We were a vast military superpower that picked fights with countries whose GDPs barely rivaled Kentucky's, yet our population abandoned its right to criticize its leaders' foreign policy out of fear of being thought insufficiently supportive of the troops we sent to bomb the shit out of the tiny, backwater states of the world.

The legacy of the Watergate/Vietnam era left us shaken. So much so that when our behavior at home and abroad rightfully incurred the mocking laughter and derision of the civilized world, we actually wobbled into the turn of the century acting like *we* were the victims, like the ability to take our magisterial, imperial selves seriously had been cruelly robbed from us, as a birthright is robbed.

That was what set the stage for 9/11 to kick off such a uniquely disgusting period in our nation's history. A bumbling aggressor that had violently meddled in the affairs of distant states, assassinated and attempted to assassinate legally elected foreign politicians, supported death squads and dictators from Indonesia to Guatemala, armed international villains like chemical-bomber Saddam Hussein and the butcher Mobutu Sese Seko, and spilled industrial poisons and toxins into ass-end-of-nowhere villages from Bhopal to Colombia, America *even before 9/11* was a country that managed nonetheless to feel sorry for itself—because we'd had to live through the Carter years. Because the whole "malaise" thing prevented us from getting our freak on in Nicaragua! Because Chevy Chase made jokes about Gerald Ford! Because somebody robbed us of our *pride!*

Well, America said after 9/11, no more! The whole terrorism thing made us insufferable on two fronts: it increased our utterly crazy sense of victimhood, while vastly expanding the scope of our aggression. It was already something like consensus before 9/11 that the SUPPORT OUR TROOPS Prime Directive meant that our military adventures could not be questioned; after 9/11, it was basically considered treasonous to pose such questions. And the woe-is-us, weepy-victim bullshit that any citizen of a country with

real problems wouldn't have thought possible in an obesely wealthy, armed-to-the-teeth empire like America became a similarly obligatory part of all public utterances, whether from self-pitying politicians like George Bush or from asshole columnists like George Will and Thomas Friedman who vowed vengeance against those terrible monsters who stole our innocence on that fateful day.

During this time David Rees was the only sane voice in all of America. He was the only one who called out the heroic "War on Terrorism" for the insane farce that it was, and is. Even the title of his strip, *Get Your War On,* hit right at what was most sordid about the whole phenomenon: the fact that we used the attacks by a small, isolated group of cave-dwelling lunatics as an excuse to revel, gleefully, in the possibilities of violent response. We set our designers to work cooking up oodles of flashy TV graphics for the inevitable military campaign; we hired Madison Avenue consultants to help the Pentagon develop catchy mission names. We cried on *Oprah!* when asked how bad 9/11 made us feel—and shed tears, in advance, for the brave boys we were now sure to lose, even if all the target countries could not exactly be decided upon right away.

In other words, we were *stoked.* As David put it, Operation Enduring Our Freedom was in the motherfucking house. He got right to the root of what was grossest about us. In countries that have been around longer than a few hundred years, in places that have suffered through more than one real tragedy, nobody throws parties when they suffer terrorist attacks or other disasters. They cart off the dead, chalk it up in the bummer column, and move on. But not America. America was going to make a big deal out of this! If you weren't American, you were never going to hear the end of how much we suffered! And if you dared to suggest that you ever suffered as much as we did, you could get ready to bend over and endure our motherfucking freedom!

For years after 9/11, every time you turned on the television, people sounded like David's GYWO strips. Or, at least, the psychic subtext of what they were saying sounded like those strips, if you happened to be listening for the psychic subtext. The actual strips captured the wallowing-in-victimhood instinct in a far funnier way. In this one, already bored with the possibilities of self-pity offered by 9/11, David's clip-art characters dreamily fast-forward to *future* possibilities for self-pity:

Sitting black clip-art guy: Those fucking goddamned terrorists! They want to blow up the Brooklyn Bridge? Why, so I can't stroll across it and look at the mutilated skyline and contemplate the mass grave their friends left for us?

Standing white clip-art guy: How much do you wanna bet that if terrorists blow up the Statue of Liberty, France won't even OFFER to replace it?

Get Your War On is a strange world where the clip-art characters alternate between a sane voice that is clearly that of the author ("You know, this Enron shit wouldn't be so bad if the politicians just finally fucking admitted that when they invoke religion in their speeches, they're totally bullshitting!") and a less sane voice that seems to represent David's exaggerated idea of what *other* Americans think and feel about the great War on Terrorism ("I just got a call that *another* one of my stepbrothers is joining the Marines! It's getting so that I start crying every time the fucking phone rings!"). The strip's frantic internal dialogue feels like a desperate attempt by the author to reconcile himself to the reality of his situation—like he wants to believe this stuff isn't happening all around him, but every time he checks, it still is.

Much has been made of David's use of clip-art pictures for the strip's distinctive look. I remember asking him about that once and I'm pretty sure he gave me some kind of answer, but I've forgotten what that was. But here's my theory on why they work so well: that's what we modern Americans look like. We're not funky, idiosyncratic caricatures with ragged edges and distinctive personalities, like the people in Crumb's strips. We don't look like the people in *The Brady Bunch* and we don't resemble hokey fifties send-ups like the people in *Happy Days* or *Laverne and Shirley*. In the sixties, seventies, even the eighties, we still had personality in this country, but these days . . .

These days we really are a bunch of static, soulless cardboard figurines, mass-produced by cookie-cutter, with two television sets for parents. The only thing distinctive about any of us is which demographic we belong to, and if you have that info, that is usually enough to explain how we'll vote, what we'll buy, and what TV shows we'll quote during dinner. Push those demographic particulars aside, though, and you'll find a nearly uniform attitude of dumb patriotism, xenophobia, and political echolalia—interchangeable humans with vague cosmetic differences mounted on identical political chassis.

That is why it makes so much sense to create a world where the characters, if they had names at all, would have names like *18-34 yr-old African-American service-industry female at bar* and *White college-educated professional male on telephone*. I don't know if David was thinking that, but it's one reason the strip works. The total indifference to individual personality and makeup, the infuriatingly unchanging landscape of cubicle phone calls and kitchenette "socializing" sessions—these are both on-target rips at what we call "community" and "life" in modern America.

But none of this would work if it weren't for the felicitous fact that David is, himself, somewhat insane. One of the things that makes *Get Your War On* so brilliant and raw is that the artist has such a beautifully tortured relationship to his own work. Almost without fail, when David is trying to be funny, his strips come off angry; when he's trying to be angry, his strips come off funny. I thought it was particularly hilarious when recent GYWO strips devolved into long screeds about drinking water in Halabja and other Iraqi reconstruction failures, rants that spread across all three panels and left David's "funny" clip-art guys with no room for a punch line, which they themselves called a "tragedy." I think David was trying to soften the rantish-ness of the Halabja bit with the little joke about the lost punch-line, but it came off like he was pissed about having to stick a "funny" comic strip under his rant, which to me was actually the biting and funny part.

The whole history of the strip is like that. The constant interplay between David's amazing, *where-the-hell-did-that-come-from?* one-liners (I remember nearly choking on a gulp of soda when I read David's description of Dennis Miller as a satirist "whose grasp of foreign policy is as strong and sure as a baby's grip on a buttered anvil") and his expletive-filled explosions of white-hot outrage comprise the real "storyline" of *Get Your War On*: it's a tale of a guy pacing back and forth in his pajamas in his New York home, trying to find his way back to humor, only to keep getting dragged back down by disgust and mortification over the state of things in "War on Terrorism" America.

It is an honest portrait of who we were, written in a time when no one else had the guts to tell us the truth about ourselves. *Get Your War On* exposes us as the cowardly, self-pitying, half-educated violence addicts that we are—and exposes the "War on Terrorism" as a pathetic excuse to cosmetically enhance our flagging self-esteem, a national boob job that didn't come close to looking real and will only look worse as we get older.

Get Your War On

October 9, 2001

October 9, 2001

October 9, 2001

October 9, 2001

October 9, 2001

October 9, 2001

So, are you down with the War On Terrorism? It's gonna be a total success!

Of course I'm down with it! My fucking son's inner-city school is gonna be fucking paying for it!

What, you mean it's not gonna pay for itself?

October 9, 2001

If you could say one thing to God right now, what would it be?

I think I would say, "Thank You, God, for Your healing gift of religion." What about you?

I'd say, "God, I regret to inform You that U.S. policy now dictates we bomb the fuck out of You up in Heaven."

Oh! I'd also say, "Monotheistic religion has always brought out the best in us humans; thank You so much for the idea of a vengeful supernatural entity who rewards people in the afterlife! That shit makes *a lot* of sense!"

October 9, 2001

I don't even know what to wish for in this fucking war! Should I wish for the destruction of militant Islam, or is wishing for the destruction of Afghanistan sufficient?

Start small. For instance, I've decided to wish for the following: *That every dumbfuck who bought a Nostradamus book since September 11th be dumped in an internment camp*, as they obviously pose a grave threat to U.S. intelligence.

Who's buying those Nostradamus books, anyway? *Atheists*? Nostradamusism freaks me out even more than fundamentalism! Let's hope the U.S. never has to battle *that* motherfucker!

October 9, 2001*

October 14, 2001

October 14, 2001

October 14, 2001

Panel 1 (Row 1): If there's one thing I love to see, it's a huge fuckin' SUV tooling through midtown Manhattan with an American flag flying half-mast on its antenna! What could be less French?

Panel 2 (Row 1): That's right! Supersize the grief! When we get our grief on, we grieve harder than *anyone!* Motherfuckers just can't grieve like the USA!

Panel 3 (Row 1): Now the world knows how the BIG DAWGS grieve! Who wants to grieve with the big dawgs? Afghanistan, do you like grieving with the big dawgs? Iraq, you can get your little flags ready! (Actually, does anyone other than Saddam Hussein even *get* to own a fucking over there?)

October 14, 2001*

Panel 1 (Row 2): Whenever I feel depressed, I take solace in my favorite corporate condolences ad— Phillips 66, in the New York Times! *It's written from the perspective of angels up in heaven.*

Panel 2 (Row 2): *"May you feel our arms around you this day and every other. . . You should see the light burning in your hearts. Sincerely, The Angels who keep you."* Hmmm.

Panel 3 (Row 2): Ahhh. . . the Angels who speak to us via petroleum companies! What a bunch of patronizing motherfu—Wait a minute—*are the angels speaking to us supposed to be dead people from the World Trade Center?* What the good fucking goddamn hell are those Phillips 66 bastards getting at?

October 14, 2001

Panel 1 (Row 3): Hey, are you on CNN.com? They've got a really interesting poll; they ask "Is al Qaeda sending coded messages to followers via video statements?" You can answer "Yes" or "No!"

Panel 2 (Row 3): What about "How the fuck would I know?" Who's qualified to answer a goddamn poll about *coded video statements?* Any American who bothers to answer that poll probably masturbates to Tom Clancy novels!

Panel 3 (Row 3): Wow! *100,000 responses!*

October 14, 2001

Holy fuck—anthrax in New York City! We're getting our fucking *ass* kicked!

Seriously! Who the fuck are we fighting, fucking *Lex Luthor*? When is the goddamn Death Star gonna shoot that big-ass laser at us?

I know! What's next—George W. Bush is gonna hold a press conference and fuckin' rip his face off and it's gonna be *Ming the Merciless* up under there? Jesus!

October 14, 2001

You know, us bombing Afghanistan isn't doing shit, *except for somehow releasing anthrax throughout America!* Can we just fucking surrender or something? Fuck *Operation: Enduring Freedom*, I want some *Operation: My Ass Enduring Without Anthrax!*

For real! So Osama bin Laden becomes our president—so what? All of a sudden I'm not allowed go to read or go to work and men throw acid at me if they can see my face? Shit, that's better than *anthrax!*

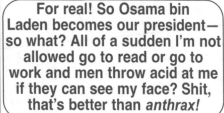

I want to take out a full-page ad in the newspaper: *Dear Whoever is Mailing All the Anthrax All Over the Place—You can be my ruler! Now can I please just for-swear alcohol and denounce Israel or whatever so I can fucking open my credit card offers without thinking my organs are gonna turn inside-out?*

October 14, 2001

Maybe I should write a poem about my feelings since September 11th; that might help! What rhymes with "alcohol-saturated dread?"

Dad, why are you calling me at work? Huh? Oh, I don't know. . . How about "alcohol, match your hated bed?" Like, you hate your bed now because of the nightmares, so you put a match to it and burn it? Well hell, Dad, I can't come up with shit just like *that!*

~~Alcohol-saturated dread~~
~~Dramatic self-medication increaseth~~
~~I'm starting to look like a damn ghost~~
~~A widower learns of gentle heroin~~
~~Visions of despair, illusions of hope~~

October 30, 2001

October 30, 2001

October 30, 2001

October 30, 2001

Panel 1: Are the bombs we've been dropping in Afghanistan for the past four weeks fucking *hollow*? The Taliban are still rocking like a hurricane!

Panel 2: Two words, my friend: *Fucking invincible.*

Panel 3: You know, I wouldn't have even noticed, but then Ashcroft said everyone had to go into a "Heightened Awareness" and in my "Heightened Awareness" I became "Highly Aware" that our bombs aren't cutting the mustard! Let's declare war on some foes *who aren't immortal,* for fuck's sake! If the Taliban had our firepower, they would have conquered Earth by now! Those motherfuckers would be waging *jihad* on Mars!

October 30, 2001

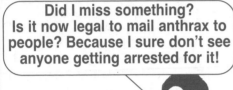

Panel 1: Did I miss something? Is it now legal to mail anthrax to people? Because I sure don't see anyone getting arrested for it!

Panel 2: I think it's only legal if you have the proper license.

Panel 3: What, like I write my letter and then I have to wait five days before I can dump a bunch of anthrax into the envelope? Fucking waiting periods! My Visa bill can't wait!

Panel 4: Waiting periods and late fees! What will they think of next? Bombs that look just like food aid packages?

October 30, 2001

Panel 1: So if you're not with us, you're against us, huh? I like it! So nice and simple! When do we start bombing western Europe?

Panel 2: Oh man! Tell the boys down at the bomb-makin' factory to brew up some coffee—they're gonna be working some serious goddamn overtime!

Panel 3: Can't we just build a fucking bomb *the size of the earth* and cut a hole out of the middle in the shape of The United States? Drop the motherfucker around us and take care of business once and for all?

October 30, 2001

 Why do I get the feeling that when the War on Terrorism is over we're gonna have more fucking Cipro in this country than we know what to do with?

 Why do I get the feeling that when the War on Terrorism is over we're gonna have more fucking impoverished citizens in this country than we know what to do with? We'll have to declare another War on Poverty!

 Right! And if you're not with us in the War on Poverty, you're against us! Dick Cheney, I'm calling you out, you oil industry bitch motherfucker! *I can't fucking find you or see you*, but I'm putting you on notice!

November 8, 2001

 Why won't American TV networks air Osama bin Laden's video statements? They seem. . . somehow. . . *almost newsworthy.* Is it the secret coded attack messages?

 Ha! They won't let us see his speeches because they're afraid WE'LL FUCKING DEFECT TO HIS SIDE! He's got serious leadership ability! C'mon, when bin Laden tells me the shit's about to hit the fan, I'm pretty sure something's about to get fucked! He's deranged, but at least you can take him at his word!

 Why do I keep calling this asshole? That didn't make me feel good!

November 8, 2001

 Remember that moment in Bush's speech when he said, "The Taliban *don't believe women should have health-care?*" Does that mean *I* can move to Kandahar and get some healthcare? I've already stopped shaving!

 Do you think Bush will give every American woman and girl free healthcare, just to piss off Osama bin Laden? I'd roll with that!

 Now, come on, there's gotta be a way to piss off bin Laden without *also* pissing off the evildoing motherfuckers who got you elected! Why don't we roll with some kickass *5,000-pound bombs* instead?

November 8, 2001

I can't believe Jesus and Allah are fighting again! Someone's gonna get their eye poked out!

Bah! We're living in the *21st Century*, and people *still* wage war to impress invisible super-heroes who live in outer space! I thought we would all be chilling out in solar-powered flying cars by now!

I wish the U.S. and al-Qaeda could team up to overthrow The Kingdom of Heaven! We've already teamed up to guarantee the total fucking ruination of millions of Afghan lives—why not take it to the next level? Could there be a more slammin' Holy War than declaring war on the Holy One?

November 8, 2001

Man! I like a good stiff *Operation Enduring Freedom* as much as the next guy, but I've reached my limits of understanding! All of a sudden my fucking mailman is a Hero on the Front Lines in the War Against Terror? My daughter wants to sell cookies to help the people my nephew's been sent to fucking *bomb?* I'm supposed to help the FBI find clues and solve crimes? I'M A CLAIMS ADJUSTER, NOT FUCK-ING ENCYCLOPEDIA BROWN! Who's in charge of this shit?

Agreed! This is totally Loony Toons— I love that the fate of the world hangs in the balance! Bush is talking about conquering evildoers, yet the CIA *can't fucking translate the evildoers' Arabic voodoo-spells!* The "Office of Homeland Security" makes the DMV look like fucking Delta Force! And, look, I understand why *bin Laden* sounds crazy— he's an eleven-foot tall motherfucker who lives in a cave! But why does Bush sound like he's addressing a fucking Dungeons & Dragons convention? At least I can tear my hair out full-time now that I've been laid off!

November 8, 2001

Hey buddy! Where the fuck have you been? I've been calling your ass for a week! We've got a lot to talk about!

Oh, man! You'll never guess *how fucking fat* I got over Thanksgiving week-end! I fucking ate like I was a refugee in a certain war-torn part of the world! It's almost 10 am—who needs a drink?

Let's drink to my hair growing back over the vacation! Now I can go to job interviews with-out looking all creepy and mutilated!

I'm back too! What rhymes with "Alcohol-saturated erosion of the Bill of Rights?"

November 29, 2001

November 29, 2001

November 29, 2001

November 29, 2001

November 29, 2001

December 12, 2001

December 12, 2001

Panel 1: I have a feeling we're gonna catch Osama bin Laden soon!

Let the games begin!

December 12, 2001

Panel 2: God, I wonder what kind of fantasies Bush is having about that? Do you think he fantasizes about publicly executing bin Laden during halftime at the Super Bowl? *What if they draw-and-quarter him?*

cough *Pay-per-view*

Panel 3: We won't be able to kill that motherfucker enough! We'll have to cryogenically freeze him after we kill him, just so we can wake his ass up to kill him again! Or develop a way to actually make a corpse *more dead* through repeated, relentless post-mortem killing. You know, kind of like what we're doing to an entire fucking country?

Panel 4: Will you fucking hurry up and kill Osama bin Laden for fuck's sake? Jesus Fucking Christ, how can I put this—YOU'VE BEEN BOMBING FOR TWO FUCKING MONTHS! WHAT THE FUCK SIZE BOMBS DO YOU NEED?

Panel 5: Serious! It's like an American bombing campaign is the elixir of eternal life for despots! Saddam Hussein will live to be four hundred years old at this rate!

Panel 6: The other good thing about an American bombing campaign is that everyone on the ground gets a super-sized Ramadan holiday! Extended fasting for all! It's like if Christmas lasted for eighty days instead of just twelve!

December 12, 2001

Panel 7: Question: How do you lose a one-eyed Muslim cleric in broad daylight?

Panel 8: The entire military might of the United States versus a cave-dwelling maniac and a one-eyed Muslim cleric! This is like Rambo versus the Hobbit!

Panel 9: After eight straight weeks of bombing, I don't like the idea of people still walking around Afghanistan! I expect some motherfuckers to be good and dead after *eight weeks*! That includes Golem and the Cyclops!

December 12, 2001

Panel 1: You know who I've come to like in all this? John Ashcroft. The guy just gives me a good feeling!

Panel 2: (no dialogue)

Panel 3: Good *God*, these are some powerful antidepressants I'm taking! *Wow!!!*

December 12, 2001

Panel 4: Have you sent out your holiday cards yet?

Panel 5: Ha! Holiday cards! First of all, anyone who didn't call to check on me after September 11th gets NO CARD! *You motherfuckers know I live in New York!* Did you just *assume* I was OK? After I saw the buildings fucking fall down? With fucking *cremated human remains* settling on my back patio, which I had to fucking wash down so I wouldn't *inhale them*? You can't send me a fucking email? While I wait for my girlfriend to fucking walk home like a goddamn refugee? If you couldn't even bother to send a fucking online animated huggy kitty cat greeting card, what makes you think I'm gonna lick a fucking stamp and send you a picture of Santa Claus or baby Jesus? *I'd rather make out with Donald Rumsfeld!*

Panel 6: Whoops! I had to put you on hold! What did you say?

December 12, 2001

Panel 7: Mullah Muhammad Omar and Osama bin Laden! Two wily motherfuckers! Who were those little phantoms in *The Family Circus* who always broke the dishes and left the house in disarray?

Panel 8: Then they'd run away and leave Billy and Jeffy standing there looking like *total* idiots!

Panel 9: "*Who organized this international terror organization? Who scribbled all over the cave?*"

NOT ME

December 12, 2001

Oh yeah! *Operation: Enduring Enron* is in the house!

Oh yeah! *Operation: Enduring Our Enron* is in the motherfucking house!

Yes! *Operation: Enduring Enron's Freedom To Make Off With A Shitload Of Money At Their Employees' Expense* is in the house!!!

January 17, 2002

I have a feeling that once I understand everything that happened with Enron, I'm gonna take off my American flag pin! I'd better take a pass on this one!

Seriously! I know Osama is my enemy! But these Enron motherfuckers were supposed to be on our side! Aren't we all on the same side here in America? Especially *now*? Shit, *I* was playing fair for Team USA!

Good ol' Team USA! Everybody working together! See how nice our leaders' friends are? My man, Kenneth Lay—*thanks for helping out, you evil prick*!

January 17, 2002

Here's what I don't understand--couldn't the evildoers at Enron have figured out a way to ruin the lives of, oh, say, al-Qaeda—*instead of their own goddamn American employees*?

Who's fucking who here? Is al-Qaeda obsessed with ruining American lives, or is Enron? Who am I supposed to want to bomb?

FUCKING BOMB TEXAS!!! They don't play fair down there! Texas is bullshit! We should sell the state to Mexico and let them fucking slaughter those assholes!

January 17, 2002

Panel 1: An Axis of Evil versus a Nation Challenged! We've got eleven fucking wars to wage all of a sudden! *Hold on, someone's at the door—*

Panel 2: Holy fucking shit, man, you'll never guess who just walked in—VOLTRON!!! Whoa! What the hell???

Panel 3: Voltron's Office of Homeland Security is in the Heeeeouse!

February 18, 2002

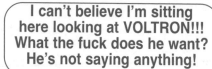

Panel 4: I can't believe I'm sitting here looking at VOLTRON!!! What the fuck does he want? He's not saying anything!

Panel 5: Isn't Voltron, like, 2,000 feet tall? How can he fit in your office?

Panel 6: The last time I thought about Voltron, I couldn't give a fuck about foreign policy! *Now I can't stop thinking about people dying all over the world!*

February 18, 2002

Panel 7: Ask Voltron what it's like battling evil! Is militarizing space gonna be cool as hell? How many bombs will it take to bring peace and justice to Earthlings?

Panel 8: I remember watching Voltron on TV with my little brother! How can I ask him about fucking insane levels of defense spending? Damn, I can't believe he's TRULY MADE OUT OF MECHANICAL LIONS!!! Oh my God!!!

Panel 9: Ask him: 20,000 bombs? 200,000 bombs? Bombs made out of robot animals or some shit like that?

February 18, 2002

February 18, 2002

February 18, 2002

February 18, 2002

What the fuck is Voltron talking about? Is this some religious thing? *Am I fucking being baptized by Voltron?*

I believe in the Human Spirit, the taker of life, who proceeds from the Father and the War. With the Father and the War it is worshipped and glorified. It has spoken through its profits. I acknowledge one War for the commission of sins. I look for no resurrection of the dead, and to the Wars of the world to come. Amen.

Sure, Voltron—Whatever you say! No need to get heavy, now! (*Dude, could you please call Office Security for me???*)

February 18, 2002

Hello? Did you ever call Office Security? I'm still knee-deep in Voltron up here!

Office Security says they now have to clear their activities with some "Tom Ridge" character! Apparently he's the mighty man who's keeping us safe now! *Funny, I never heard of the motherfucker doing anything useful!*

Hell *yes* the suspect looks foreign, Mr. Ridge! He's a robot made out of LIONS, for fuck's sake!

March 28, 2002

I wonder why Tom Ridge won't authorize the detention of Voltron? I can't be a productive member of society with his mechanical-lion ass staring at me!

Maybe the government is assigning every American their own personal Voltron! *Schweeet!* You know they've got the defense budget increase to do it!

Seriously, a permanent Voltronic chaperone would definitely make me feel safer than a fucking magical missile shield floating around in outer space!

March 28, 2002*

March 28, 2002

April 22, 2002

April 22, 2002

May 2, 2002

May 2, 2002

May 2, 2002

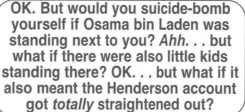

Uhh, guys? Someone from the Office of Homeland Security just called saying they "overheard" you discussing "suicide-bombing" yourselves? Could we please fucking focus on the Henderson account?

OK. But would you suicide-bomb yourself if Osama bin Laden was standing next to you? *Ahh...* but what if there were also little kids standing there? OK... but what if it also meant the Henderson account got *totally* straightened out?

What the fuck are you talking about? The whole point of getting the Henderson account straightened out is the cash bonus I'll get (which'll be going straight into my stamp collection, thank you very much)! Hang up the phone and get back to work!

May 2, 2002*

OK, one last scenario: Say we somehow LOST the War on Terror, and the Taliban fucking invaded New York and kicked you out of your apartment. Now you're living in a cement hovel on Staten Island. Would you suicide-bomb yourself to get your apartment back for your kids?

Dude, listen to me! I am not the suicide-bombing type! I like to hang out with my friends and relax and fuckin' listen to "smooth jazz." MAYBE I would throw some rocks from Staten Island, but I'm not about to go fuckin' *explode myself!* I don't want total strangers picking up my goddamn strewn-about body parts— I don't even like having my picture taken!

What the fuck is wrong with me???

May 2, 2002

I just got a call that *another* one of my step-brothers is joining the Marines. It's getting so that I start crying every time the fucking phone rings!

Damn! Is your family gonna personally overthrow Saddam Hussein? Heh!

Well hell, what was I supposed to say? I can't relate to her shit! My parents fucking paid for me to take an SAT prep course! You think I was gonna join the Marines???

May 2, 2002

Goddamn! I'm sick of these fake-ass terror alerts!

Me too! Don't tell me "there's definitely going to be an attack–*within two years*." I can figure that shit out for myself!

My boss asked me, "Do you think the White House is trying to distract people from asking questions about intelligence failures?" I said, "All I know is, if I'm not running for my goddamn life within two weeks, I'm gonna be plenty pissed!"

May 22, 2002

You know what's sort of weird? Dick Armey openly called for ethnic cleansing and nobody seemed to care! Can I openly call for some secret fantasies of my own? I mean, they might be freaky, but they're not goddamn ETHNIC CLEANSING!

Cute!

I used to feel ashamed about flipping off other drivers. . . but you know what? It's not like I'm OPENLY CALLING FOR THEIR ETHNIC CLEANSING! So fuck it!

This frank, open, discussion of the benefits of ETHNIC CLEANSING by a major American politician kind of makes me feel less guilty about not paying my taxes!

May 22, 2002

These fucking goddamn terrorists! They want to to blow up the Brooklyn Bridge? Why, so I can't walk across it and look at the destroyed Manhattan skyline and contemplate the fucking *mass grave* their friends left for us?

How much do you wanna bet that if terrorists blow up the Statue of Liberty, the French won't even OFFER to replace it?

–Wait, hold up. *Just how interesting could that children's book have been?* What would it have taken to get Bush to put the fucking book down immediately that morning? Maybe if someone fucking *flew the World Trade Center into the Pentagon?* Would that have been serious enough?

May 22, 2002

My girlfriend and I just drove across America to get married in Las Vegas. We went to Kansas for the first time; crossed the Rio Grande Gorge; touched the Four Corners; listened to Najavo radio; and watched the sun set over the Grand Canyon.

Outside Las Vegas, traffic slowed to a mind-numbing crawl over the Hoover Dam because of a July 4th terror alert. We were 24 hours away from getting married, inching across the dam, hoping not to get blown up.

When we rolled into Las Vegas, we thought we had reached the Promised Land. The old hotel signs were so beautiful, and we were still alive, and sunburnt, and—*why am I telling you this? I don't even know you! I'm a temp!*

Sweat much?

Summer, 2002

Did you have a good vacation, under God?

I did, thanks, under God. Are you ready to have a good war with Iraq under God?

As ready as I'll ever be, I guess, under God. Do we really have a choice under God?

July 11, 2002

Billions of blue blistering barnacles! I totally forgot we were waging a war in Afghanistan until we. . . bombed the "Under God" out of some innocent locals.

War in Af*wherethe-fuck*istan? The war I'm following is Bush's War Against Unethical Business Leaders! It's about to get *serious*! Just about as serious as a war against your own best friends and life-sustaining support network can get.

It's getting so I don't even know which War to Get My On first! (Though I always start with my personal War Against Joe "Under God" Lieberman, for luck.)

*July 11, 2002**

Aren't you tired of all the newspaper photos of ~~dead Afghan civilians~~ American stockbrokers holding their heads in their hands?

People laugh at me for keeping my money in a big tin bucket. Well you know what? A big tin bucket is not gonna fucking *lie to me* about its financial performance!

Is that because a big tin bucket doesn't think it's entitled to do whatever the hell it wants, just because its asinine peer group is running the country?

July 11, 2002

So I just signed up for two classes: "*How To Set Up Your Telephone Service*" and "*How To Deliver Your Own Goddamn Mail.*" Operation TIPS is gonna result in me learning how to do everything myself—I'll just let Ashcroft know if I uncover anything TERRORIST-RELATED about myself.

I always thought it was called "Operation TIPSY." That's been my personal operation since last fall. I combine it with "Operation Everybody Loves Raymond."

My nephew said, "The meter reader is supposed to SPY on me to find out if I'm a terrorist? If America is really gonna play 'Behind the Iron Curtain,' there better be some *fine* fuckin' state-subsidized alcohol! And our powerlifting team better kick ass!"

July 11, 2002*

Do you ever get the feeling that a secret game is being played in America, and nobody will tell you the rules?

Huh? Are you in "code-mode?"

When I heard Halliburton was contracted to build new prisons in Guantanamo Bay, I got really excited—like, "Oh my God, they're finally showing us how to play the game! Put me in, coach!"

I'm dying over here on the bench! Jesus God in heaven, PLEASE let me at least fucking carry the bats for these guys! I mean, they'd look after their batboy, right?

August 7, 2002

I know what you mean. I used to think Congress would be a good team to play for. Then I watched them run to the steps of the Capitol to recite the Pledge of Allegiance, yelling out "Under God!" like the MOST annoying kid in Sunday School—like, who are you trying to impress, the *Devil*? FUCKING GET BACK TO WORK AND KEEP TRACK OF OUR WARS!

That's when I realized Congress is strictly farm league shit. They'd probably have a bald eagle-fucking contest, if they thought it would impress us.

Right! Whereas Dick Cheney? He's not trying to impress me. He's just minding his business. *And that's why he will be the last man walking the scorched, post-apocalyptic earth.*

God will fly down to pour the Gatorade on him.

August 7, 2002

When I read that the State Department doesn't want to interfere with a killing- and torture- and raping spree sponsored by Indonesia's *official fucking military* because doing so would incon-venience *Exxon Mobil*, I *knew* this War on Terrorism was "for real!"

Don't be dumb! If we ask Exxon Mobil to shut down a killing- and torture- and raping spree enjoyed by their security forces, the Chinese might drum up more business in Indonesia!

I wonder what would happen if you literally had to fill up your gas tank with the bones of killed and raped people in order to make your car run?

August 7, 2002

Say, did you hear about the "Killing- and Torture- and Raping Spree Party" that Exxon Mobil is hosting in Indonesia? It's rape-a-rific!

Aaarghh! And here I am stuck at my office's stupid summer pot luck! It's torture, I tell you! Well, OK, not *actual* torture—at least, not like getting tortured, and then raped, and then killed. But the potato salad *does* seriously suck.

Hey, Mr. Sarcastic, what's the matter? Don't you like The War On Terrorism? ~~Exxon Mobil's~~ We're winning!

August 7, 2002

August 7, 2002

August 18, 2002 (Epilogue to first GYWO book)

NOTE: I uncovered these classic *Get Your War On* cartoons in my attic. They were made in the 1980s, when I was young and naive. The drawing, grammar, and typography of these strips are a bit crude, but they offer valuable context for today's foreign policy kerfuffles.

September 27, 2002

Well, it's been over a year and the president still can't seem to get around to FUCKING FIRING SOMEONE for the September 11th attacks!

I mean, was that somehow NOT the most colossal fucking fuck-up imaginable? I don't care if you fucking retroactively fire someone from the Roosevelt administration—just let me know that if I can get fired for (*ahem*) stealing coffee filters from the office kitchenette, some motherfuckers in the government can get fired when THREE THOUSAND AMERICANS are murdered in one morning!!! I'm supposed to trust you to wage new wars whenever you want, so fucking start acting like you take this shit seriously!

Saddam Hussein is DEAD MEAT!

September 27, 2002

Remember those leftover civilians in that country where we waged our last war a few months ago? Do they realize they're *one war away* from being completely forgotten?

Maybe the plan is to feed all the hungry Afghans using the bodies of dead Iraqis?

If that's the case, let me just say one thing: I hope leftover Iraqis enjoy the taste of North Koreans!

September 27, 2002

This War Against Saddam Hussein is gonna rock *twenty* times harder than that lame War Against Terror!

What, did the War Against Terror not sufficiently rock you? Remember when we allowed al-Qaeda to escape into Pakistan?

Yeah! And remember when. . . ah, fuck—who am I kidding? I can't remember a goddamn thing about the last twelve months! Did we win yet?

September 27, 2002

Remember the good ol' days, when the biggest threats to the Homeland were 2 Live Crew recordings?

Me so war-ny! Me bomb you long time!

November 5, 2002

Henry Kissinger? Jesus Christ, are we fucking MOVING BACKWARDS IN TIME???

It's always a comfort to see Kissinger standing beside a U.S. president. Putting him in charge of the 9/11 probe is like putting Robert Mugabe in charge of the Department of Agriculture.

Does Bush even know who these motherfuckers *are?* Didn't he get suspicious when he saw Kissinger and John Poindexter licking the blood off each other's hands?

November 26, 2002*

Well, at least Timmy had a good ten years without having to know who Henry Kissinger was.

There's something so precious about a young child's first encounter with Henry Kissinger. At least it takes their mind off terror threats and Saddam Hussein.

Mommeee! Who's the scary old man in the bad suit standing at the podium with President Bush? And why is there a huge pile of skulls and dead bodies all around him?

November 26, 2002

I can't remember—when Kissinger signs a U.S. government paycheck, does he use a ballpoint pen, or the bloody, severed limb of an East Timorese child?

What, you can't stand the taste of a little medium-rare realpolitik every once in a while? You'd prefer a vegetarian foreign policy, waged with watercress and asparagus? Good luck building muscle mass, Urkel.

Huh. So is John Poindexter still developing that breakfast cereal called "Lying-sack-of-shit-felon-O's?"

November 26, 2002

"An Open Letter To The Pentagon, Concerning Their Recent Sacking Of Linguists Specializing In Arabic, Allegedly Due To Their Being Homosexual"

Dear Pentagon: How do you say "*Are you fucking insane?*" in Arabic?

P.S. If that joke is already old, I have another one: How do you say, "*I can't believe we're paying you one billion dollars a day to piss on the grave of Mark Bingham—I feel safer already, you sick motherfuckers,*" in Arabic?

November 26, 2002

Holy shit! The southern states are seceding!

I heard they're even gonna print up their own money! HA! Stupid, fake-ass Southern money!

Maybe they can use their fuckin' fake money to rebuild Atlanta after we burn it to the ground!

January 4, 1861

May 11, 1863

January 15, 2003*

January 19, 2003

January 19, 2003

January 19, 2003

*January 19, 2003**

January 19, 2003

January 19, 2003*

January 20, 2003

February 10, 2003

February 10, 2003

February 10, 2003

February 10, 2003

February 10, 2003

February 10, 2003*

February 14, 2003

February 26, 2003

March 10, 2003

Why does George W. Bush get everything he wants? Is it because he prays for it?

What are you talking about? Didn't you see the press conference? He prays for peace, my anonymous clip-art co-worker, he *prays for peace*— and he's sure not getting *that*. (Hey, Mr. Bush, how does it feel to *want?* Oh—never mind.)

Dear Mr. Bush: PRAY HARDER, FOR FUCK'S SAKE! My mom can't do it all on her own!!! *Are you praying in a sarcastic voice or something?*

March 10, 2003

Someday, when I'm driving through a reconstructed, democratic Baghdad in my Freedom Car, I will pause and ask, Did the U.S. Government say *one true thing* in justifying Operation <insert <u>the tough-ass name that we will soon learn</u> here>?

And I will look up from counting ballots in Syria to reply, Who fuckin' cares? It worked out, didn't it?

And I will have to admit: *It did indeed.* (Then I'll probably have to get out and stop an Iraqi child from lapping up the water dripping from my Freedom Car's muffler. Why are those kids so thirsty?)

March 10, 2003

Freedom Fries? Fuckin' *Freedom Fries???* OK, I have a question—is the War on Terrorism over? Because I sure as hell want to know that ALL THE TERRORISTS IN THE WORLD HAVE BEEN CAPTURED before legislators actually take the time to rename their GODDAMN CAFETERIA FOOD! Listen: They're called French Fries, they're greasy, and they taste good with mayonnaise! FUCKIN' DEAL WITH IT!!!

You know what the worst thing about "Freedom Fries" is? It just proves that nobody is taking this shit seriously. FOR FUCK'S FUCKING SAKE, we're about to go to war AGAIN! Would somebody please act like a fucking goddamn grown-up for once???

Why, is there something at stake all of a sudden?

*March 10, 2003**

March 10, 2003

March 20, 2003

March 20, 2003

March 20, 2003

March 20, 2003

March 20, 2003

Panel 1: All I have to say is, once this is over, the Iraqi people better be the *freest fucking people on the face of the earth.* They better be freer than *me.* They better be so fucking free they can *fly.*

Panel 2: And they better get *fed.* They better get totally chubby. I want a fuckin' five-mile-long buffet for those kids—and I want that buffet to be *permanent.*

Panel 3: And I want a multi-million dollar reconstruction contract for Halliburton. God, that would really be so. . . *just.*

March 20, 2003

Panel 4: Just promise me one thing. Promise me that when you hear Saddam Hussein is dead, you'll stop moaning about this war for a moment and think of all the people that odious motherfucker killed. Raise a glass to his victims.

Panel 5: You know what? Don't give me that shit. *I know when to grieve, and who for.* Those sanctions made Saddam stronger and his victims weaker. Yet, somehow, *mentioning this fact to people over the years* made me a "hippie." A HIPPIE? I'm a middle manager who lifts weights and doesn't like the smell of marijuana! Meanwhile, Donald Rumsfeld is about to be treated as a humanitarian liberator! You don't need to tell me who to "raise a glass to," you fucking idiot— I raise six glasses every night, just to get drunk enough to love this country like I did as a kid: without feeling like it's *using me.*

Panel 6: Come on, I was trying to have a moment!

March 20, 2003

Panel 7: The Coalition of the Willing is about to rock! Thanks, Uzbekistan! Thanks, Macedonia! You guys are the best!

Panel 8: Can you believe Afghanistan signed on? Do they really have time to help with this?

Panel 9: Oh, that's no big deal— they're just allowing us the use of some broken promises.

March 20, 2003

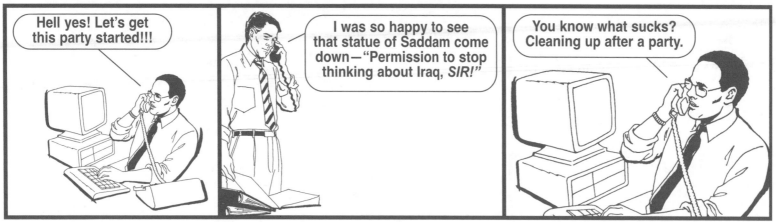

April 9, 2003

April 9, 2003

April 9, 2003

April 9, 2003

April 9, 2003

April 9, 2003

April 9, 2003

April 24, 2003

The GYWO Players in:"Have You Seen My Book of Virtues?"

May 8, 2003

Hello, is this Trireme Partners? How'd I get your number? Uhhh. . . I just looked under "World's Skankiest Venture Capital Fund" in the Yellow Pages. Yellow's the color of fear, right?

Listen, may I please speak to Richard Perle? It's regarding my missing Book of Virtues. I thought maybe he had it.

He wiped his *WHAT* with it???

May 8, 2003

Hey, as long as I have you on the phone, can I ask you a question? Is it true Henry Kissinger sits on your advisory board?

Wow. Oh, believe me, I wish Kissinger would sit on *my* advisory board! He's so famous! I was sad when he quit the 9/11 investigation. He would have brought real "Book of Virtues" integrity to it. :-)

Seriously, though—aren't you guys worried about ghosts?

May 8, 2003

Yeah, I read that Business-Week article too! Kissinger's quote was, "*We try to serve our country. How the hell are we supposed to make a living?*"

I know, the words "Kissinger" and "living" sound kind of strange together, huh?

—And he quit the 9/11 investigation *precisely because* "to serve our country" would have jeopardized his financial interests! Jesus, *when* will he go to the ninth word in his quote? Do some Americans actually still walk on the same side of the street as him?

May 8, 2003

Panel 1: Why aren't you at work? You think just because Ari Fleischer, Christie Whitman, and Tommy Franks are calling it quits, you can too?

Panel 2: Whoa—*what if the three of them quit because they're starting a band together*? Talk about a—

Panel 3: I got laid off. I'm standing in my kitchen wearing *pleated shorts!* And, by God, if we haven't invaded Iran by the time my checking account balance hits zero, there's gonna be a problem.

May 30, 2003

Panel 4: Please, buddy. Just remember what Jay Garner said before he was dethroned as King of Iraq: "*We ought to be beating our chests every day. We ought to look in a mirror and be proud, and stick out our chests and suck in our bellies, and say: Damn, we're Americans!*"

Panel 5: Yeah, it's real easy to look in a mirror and be proud when you're wearing pleated shorts. And you know what's really pathetic? I don't even have any dividends to get tax-decreased. When'll they cut taxes on not-having-health-insurancends?

Panel 6: Don't worry—I'm such a loser I don't know what a dividend even *is*. When they start cutting taxes on shit I can't *define*, I know it's time to start buying condensed milk. *Goddamn lumpy-ass milk.*

May 30, 2003

Panel 7: So you need work, eh? Why don't you become a professional REVISIONIST HISTORIAN?

Panel 8: You know how I like my revisionist history! And I keep thinking I'm gonna get away with it, but President Bush keeps catching me on it!

Panel 9: "*Revisionist History*" just means "*Ending a sentence about justifications for the Iraq war with a question mark instead of nine exclamation points,*" right?

May 30, 2003

June 5, 2003

June 5, 2003

June 5, 2003

 Knock knock!

 Who's there?

 WEAPONS OF MASS DESTRUCTION!

 So *there* you are!

 Knock knock!

 Who's there?

 Afghanistan!

 Who?

June 5, 2003

 *Vroom, vroom!* Outta my way! I've got the pedal to the metal, driving the ROAD MAP TO PEACE! *Honk, honk!* Israeli settlers, time to pull up stakes and move the fuck out! Palestinian suicide bombers, time to keep your goddamn explosions to yourselves!

 I'm so glad that Pat Robertson is sharing his views on the road map with Washington: "*If they do anything other than make Jerusalem the capital of Israel, they would be messing with the word and the power of God.*" Hey, Pat, is 9/11 still the fault of atheists and lesbians, you fucking INSANE RELIGIOUS PRICK? Why is this guy allowed to weigh in on *anything*? (PS: "*Messing*"? What, are we poking God with a stick?)

 When I saw Bush standing with Abbas and Sharon on the banks of Aqaba, my first thought was, "Where's the banner with ten-foot-tall monosyllabic words printed on it? How am I supposed to know what to feel???"

Seriously, though: Good luck, everyone!

June 5, 2003

 Whew! I just flew in from Burma, and lemme tell ya, my arms sure are tired—from enslaving people to work on Unocal's pipeline! Oh—and also from raping those who disobey me!

 Mmm. . . *slave labor*. You know the best thing about slave labor? It's free.

 Man, that better be one hell of a pipeline Unocal's got. It better pipe the greatest goddamn gasoline of all time! Holy shit, though—you don't suppose the gasoline could actually jump out of my gas tank and rape *me*?

Cartoonist's note: As of this cartoon, it is only alleged that Unocal supported the use of slave labor, rape, and torture in building its Yadana pipeline. However, it is definitely true that the U.S. Justice Department (*my* Justice Department, for God's sake) is trying to dismiss a lawsuit seeking damages for this alleged slave labor. Mmm. . . *alleged slave labor*. Where can I buy me some stock in that?

June 18, 2003

July 2, 2003

August 12, 2003

"Killing You is a Very Easy Thing For Us": Human Rights Abuses in Southeast Afghanistan (Human Rights Watch, 2003) *August 12, 2003*

August 19, 2003

August 19, 2003

August 19, 2003

And lemme say something to whoever blew up the UN building in Iraq: What the fuck are you doing? We're trying to *fucking feed you*, you fucking freaks!

You motherfuckers really want to live in a country with no electricity and no food? THEN MOVE TO NORTH KOREA! Hell, we could probably pay you to invade. Would you like that, you stupid ideological maniac fucks?

Wouldn't it be awesome if this bombing made the UN totally flip out? What if the UN sent 500,000 soldiers with blue helmets into Iraq and they went on a total killing rampage? *Then* would Donald Rumsfeld respect 'em?

August 19, 2003

For a few weeks, I was actually trying to keep up with who said what when about the Iraq war. I thought it would be interesting to rank everyone using my Mendacity Index.

But then I said, *You know what? I don't care if people are being less than 500% truthful with me. Fuck it*—I LIKE BEING LED. And sometimes, being led is worth being lied to.

Uh-oh! Something tells me you're not gonna like the birthday present I ordered for you. . .

OK, who's gonna sign for this Z-90 Bullshit Detector?

Aren't you afraid it'll overheat?

August 19, 2003

Wouldn't it be weird if in twenty years Iraq had a functioning Social Security system, but America didn't?

Wouldn't it be cool if in twenty years America's deficit *actually became self-aware* and started crushing every nation in its path?

Our only hope is that in twenty years America's deficit will have grown so fuckin' big it literally develops *life-giving teats* senior citizens can suckle, instead of receiving Medicare.

August 19, 2003

August 19, 2003

August 19, 2003

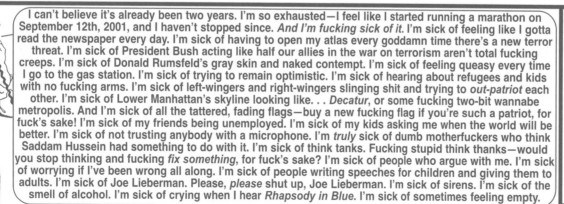

August 19, 2003 (September 11, 2003)

September 15, 2003

October 1, 2003

October 8, 2003*

Panel 1: Aren't you glad the smoking gun never came in the form of a mushroom cloud?

Panel 2: I never understood that line—was Condoleezza Rice talking about a smoking gun in the form of a mushroom cloud over *Iraq*, or over *us*? The idea of Saddam Hussein flying over here and dropping a nuclear bomb on us seems fuckin' *retarded*.

Panel 3: My friend in the State Department told me, "If you see what looks like a mushroom cloud over Iraq, don't worry—it's not the smoking gun. It's just Ahmad Chalabi blowing more smoke out of his ass."

October 20, 2003

Panel 1: Come on, admit it—aren't you a little psyched things are going so bad in Iraq?

Panel 2: You want me to admit I hate Bush more than I care about Iraqis? Call me back in ten whiskey sours.

Panel 3: So you're sitting in your chair gloating while other people's bodies are torn apart. That's a good citizen. When you pledge allegiance to nihilism, what do you put your hand over?

Panel 4: Gimme a fucking break! First of all, you know me—I don't sit. Second, why should I cheer for a team that fucking *lied to me* just to get me in the stadium? And now I've gotta pay for my seat *and* their friends' salaries? Meanwhile, they haven't even finished the *first* game they started playing! The whole franchise is totally fucked up!

October 28, 2003

Panel 1: Since the smoking gun didn't come in the form of a mushroom cloud, what form will the smoking gun come in?

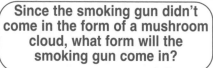

Panel 2: The smoking gun will come in the form of a completely disassembled gun that is not smoking, because it exists only in the form of a future potential possibility of creating the conditions that may eventually lead to the assembly of the gun which may one day smoke. *At which point you may die.*

Panel 3: You mean *die of boredom*, waiting for a goddamn real smoking gun?

October 21, 2003

Panel 1 (November 6, 2003):

Do you feel safer now that Saddam Hussein has been overthrown?

Panel 2:

Actually, you know what makes me feel *real* safe? Knowing that Donald Rumsfeld and Dick Cheney can get anything they want, no matter what. Even a war. That's *bad-ass*.

I've never gotten a single war I wanted!

Panel 3:

We can put a man on the moon; we can make the biggest damn cars in the world; and we can invade countries for mythical reasons. America dwells in the Age of Wizardry.

Excelsior!

Panel 4:

Later...

I thought of another cool thing about America in the Age of Wizardry: When our soldiers die, they turn invisible. I used to think only Iraqi civilians had that power!

November 6, 2003

Panel 1 (November 15, 2003):

Jesus, how can I not know anyone who's been killed yet? How long will that last?

Panel 2:

And how come I've never written a letter to my Representative about anything?

Panel 3:

I'm thankful I'm surrounded by more life than death.

Panel 4:

Oh! And that there's no god to see how pathetic I am.

November 15, 2003

Panel 1 (December 9, 2003):

Can you believe John Kerry said he didn't expect Bush to "f--- it up as badly as he did?" Holy f---!

Panel 2:

Hey! Watch the language!

Panel 3:

And now the f---in' White House is criticizing Kerry's language? What, the motherf---ers aren't busy enough f---ing with the environment? What the f--- happened to *priorities*?

Panel 4:

DON'T YOU KNOW THAT PEOPLE WHO USE CURSE WORDS HAVE LIMITED VOCABULARIES???

December 9, 2003

Actually, why do they even f---ing care what John Kerry said in his interview? HE VOTED FOR THE F---ING WAR! WHAT THE F--- ELSE DO YOU WANT?

What, he's gotta get down on his knees and lick George W. Bush's fake f---ing flight helmet? He's gotta say Bush *didn't* f--- up the situation in Iraq?

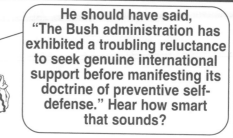

He should have said, "The Bush administration has exhibited a troubling reluctance to seek genuine international support before manifesting its doctrine of preventive self-defense." Hear how smart that sounds?

December 9, 2003

Don't you think Kerry should speak like an adult and not use bad language? There's too much ugliness in politics.

Oh, I love that! What's gonna happen— we all use too much profanity and the "national discourse" becomes so debased that we *actually launch a war in the Middle East under false pretenses, in defiance of international law, without knowing how to manage its aftermath?*

Wait. . . that sounds familiar. Were dead bodies involved?

December 9, 2003

Fuck! FUCK!!! Motherfuckin' fuckers fucking up every fuckin' thing they can get their fuckin' hands on! Fuckin' FUCKITY FUCK!!!

Whew. . . that's better.

December 9, 2003

You know the good thing about military guys? They don't bullshit. They say what they mean.

Like Lieutenant Colonel Nathan Sassaman, talking about Iraqi civilians: *"With a heavy dose of fear and violence, and a lot of money for projects, I think we can convince these people that we are here to help them."*

Oh, you *"think"* we can convince 'em, huh? You got a fuckin' heavy dose of fear and violence and you can't do better than *"think"*??? What the fuck kind of heavy dose do you use if you *don't* convince 'em?

December 9, 2003

I resented you until you hit me with that heavy dose of fear and violence! That was TOUGH!!!

I have a few more doses in my medicine cabinet, just in case.

Seriously, I *think* you're starting to convince me that you are here to help me.

Good. Because I'm going to build a military base on your lawn.

December 9, 2003

I was worried about the situation in Iraq—until good ol' *Heavy Dose of Fear and Violence* showed up!

Do think the dose will be heavy enough?

Umm. . . next year's budget for the dose is over 400 billion dollars. It should be plenty heavy.

Wouldn't it be cool if people could hear a language but not speak it?

December 9, 2003

December 14, 2003

December 15, 2003

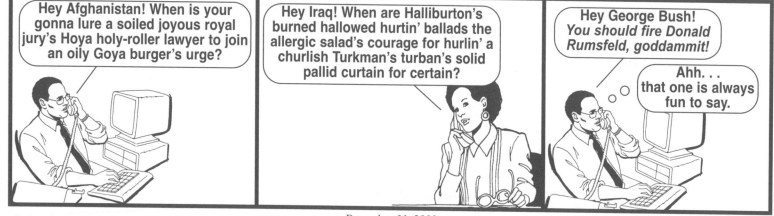

December 31, 2003

Panel 1: Guess where I'm going? I'm going to Afghanistan to register voters for their new democracy that we gave them!

Panel 2: Ooh, I wanna come! You'll only be registering voters in Kabul in broad daylight, right?

Panel 3: No, man! You gotta register everyone! I'm going into the rural provinces! I'm bringing my Walkman.

Panel 4: Oh. Then can I have your fax machine? Because you will not be coming back.

January 7, 2004

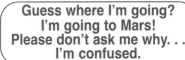

Panel 1: Guess where I'm going? I'm going to Mars! Please don't ask me why. . . I'm confused.

Panel 2: Ooh, I wanna come! Who are we fighting on Mars? Wait, lemme guess—ASTRO BIN LADEN.

Panel 3: No, this isn't about fighting terrorists! This is about pulling together as a nation and reaching for the stars and DOING THE DUMBEST GODDAMN THING IN THE WORLD. Where's my Martian flag pin?

January 14, 2004

Panel 1: You know, I remember when I was worried the war in Iraq would distract us from rebuilding Afghanistan. (Thank God I was wrong about that!)

Panel 2: Today I *literally* asked myself, "Are we gonna get distracted from rebuilding Iraq because of our mission to Mars?" Now, what the *hell* kind of president brings about a state of affairs where his citizens have to ask that question?

Panel 3: *MY* president!!!

January 14, 2004

Strip 1:

I'm starting to think the two noblest words in the English language are "FUCK NASA."

Seriously, why are we still going into space? To find out if broccoli can grow upside-down in zero gravity? WHO FUCKIN' CARES? *EVERYONE IN AFRICA IS DYING OF AIDS, FOR GOD'S SAKE!* I don't give a fuck whether albino snails can have sex in a fucking space shuttle! You need to shut down Cape Canaveral and FIX EARTH, GODDAMMIT!

Great—you not only hate America, now you gotta hate Mars too?

January 14, 2004

Strip 2:

Remember when Bush flew that fighter jet onto the aircraft carrier after we accomplished the mission?

Wouldn't it be awesome if he *landed a rocket ship* on the Capitol Dome and delivered the State of the Union speech dressed like an astronaut?

If that happens, Joe Lieberman will be sitting on the front row wearing a googly-antenna headband and wrap-around sunglasses, holding a sparkler.

January 14, 2004

Strip 3:

You know what we should do? Send up a Mars mission and then once they're up in space, call them and say, "You guys can't reenter the atmosphere until you develop a cure for AIDS. Get crackin'."

C'mon, I bet if you asked people in Africa if they wanted us to go to Mars, they'd say yes—because it's important for humanity to reach ever upward. It's inspirational. We're at our best when we dare to dream of a—

GAAAH!!! I just puked in my space helmet!

January 14, 2004

January 14, 2004

January 22, 2004

January 22, 2004

January 22, 2004*

February 2, 2004

February 9, 2004

February 13, 2004

February 16, 2004

February 23, 2004

February 27, 2004

March 2, 2004

March 8, 2004

The Defense Department is paying Ahmad Chalabi's group $340,000 a month.

Goddamn! Now *that's* some expensive bullshit!

We really couldn't find anyone to make shit up off the top of their head for cheaper than *$340,000 a month*? Jesus, wouldn't it have been cheaper just to pay a million monkeys to type random shit about Iraq on a million typewriters?

Yeah, but then you would've had a million monkeys fantasizing about being the king of Iraq, instead of just one creepy asshole.

March 11, 2004

If we're paying $340,000 a month for Ahmad Chalabi's Bullshit, it better be the greatest goddamn bullshit the world has ever seen. Does it know how to do long division and tie sailor knots and shit like that?

I mean, if you paid me $340,000 a month for *my* bullshit, I'd at least make sure it was *useful*. I know my bullshit would be able to fix your microwave or something.

For that kind of money, I expect Ahmad Chalabi's Bullshit to mop every kitchen in America and press our slacks.

Maybe after Ahmad Chalabi's Bullshit is done pressing our slacks, it could clean up some of the blood around here!

March 11, 2004

OK, pretend I'm Donald Rumsfeld. You're the BBC. Ask me if we're really gonna hand over power to the Iraqis on June 30th.

Tally-ho, wincing old chap! Will you be able to keep the June 30th date for transfer of sovereignty?

"Do I think it will happen? It has a chance of happening, yes. Will it happen for sure? Who knows? I don't know what's going to happen tomorrow."

Wow.

Donald Rumsfeld is a volunteer, right? We don't actually pay him a salary, do we?

March 23, 2004

Holy shit! Are you listening to Rumsfeld's testimony to the 9/11 commission? He's talking about Bush issuing an ultimatum to the Taliban. He says the Taliban refused, so then *"he initiated the global war on terrorism."*

I'm not a huge Bush fan, but that is one tough-ass thing to be able to say you did—"Yeah. . . so then I had to go and initiate the global war on terrorism. Wasn't no big thing."

When did Rumsfeld say, *"I'm an egomaniac who lives in an echo chamber, so then I initiated completely fucking up post-war Iraq?"*

March 23, 2004

You know what's sick? *It's probably in America's best interest if we never find Osama bin Laden.* Because as long as that motherfucker's on the run, it'll be hard to forget about Afghanistan. The sooner we forget about it, the sooner it falls apart and psychos exploit its weakness again.

You're still moaning about Afghanistan, huh? I guess you didn't hear: The road from Kabul to Kandahar has been fixed.

Give me a break! I'm so tired of hearing about that goddamn stupid road! After all this time, the best we can say is that we *paved a goddamn ROAD?* Big fuckin' deal! I stained my deck—does that make me a humanitarian?

Right. We *should* do more to help Afghanistan. I'll stimulate its economy—put me down for another fifty-pound sack of opium!

March 24, 2004

Man, the Road Map to Peace is working GREAT. It's working so great, I think the Middle East is actually getting too peaceful.

I think people in the Middle East would take us more seriously if we just renamed it the "Road Map to Excitement."

I think Central Asia is already using that road map.

April 1, 2004

Panel 1 (top row, left):
"IT'S UZBEKIKITTY! THE CUTE LITTLE KITTY WHO COULD BECOME FERAL AT ANY MINUTE!"

Watch carefully! You wouldn't want to miss any exciting developments!

Panel 2 (top row, middle):
Meow! Mr. Rumsfeld likes to pet me and give me milk! But Mr. Powell says I am a BAD KITTY!

Panel 3 (top row, right):
Say, would you please sharpen my claws? I have some *purrr*fectly legitimate scratching to do!

April 1, 2004

Panel 4 (middle row, left):
"GOOD OL' UZBEKIKITTY! THE SCARIEST GODDAMN KITTY IN TOWN!"

Purr! I'm glad we're friends, Amerikitty!

Panel 5 (middle row, middle):
You should get to know me better! I know a lot of fun things we can do together! *Meow!*

Panel 6 (middle row, right):
Ooh! Here's something we can do— I can help you fight the War on Terrorism, and you can keep your goddamn nose out of my business!

April 1, 2004

Panel 7 (bottom row, first):
Remember when certain people in the White House said Iraqis would greet us with flowers? Remind me never to request a birthday bouquet from those geniuses.

Panel 8 (bottom row, second):
I wonder if getting attacked, burned, strung up and stomped on will come to be known as receiving a "Fallujah Bouquet."

Panel 9 (bottom row, third):
You know, I'd forgive the White House for bullshitting us into war—if they'd just promise to move to Iraq and sweep up the rose petals themselves.

Panel 10 (bottom row, fourth):
Someone better tell Wolfowitz to bring a big-ass push broom!

April 12, 2004

April 16, 2004

April 16, 2004

April 16, 2004

Panel 1: You know what's weird? It's almost like, when we moved troops from Afghanistan to Iraq, we moved all our *Stay the Course* and *Stand Our Ground* too. I don't think we left a single *Stay the Course* lying around over there.

Panel 2: You know what the bottom line is? If Bush was a doctor he'd use the "get well soon" card to diagnose the illness.

Panel 3: Are you suggesting that if we're fighting a "war of ideas" in the Muslim world, we need a commander-in-chief who can successfully *express one* when he opens his mouth? I always thought the White House was just handicapping itself so the Clash of Civilizations wouldn't look fixed.

April 16, 2004

Panel 4: Complicated times call for simple language! How else do you justify being allies with Pakistan without your *goddamn head exploding from cognitive dissonance*?

Panel 5: Listen. Me *like* simple words. Make me feel STRONG, like "Hulk SMASH!" But simple words plus geopolitical strategy contingent on morally compromised transnational alliances not so great. Maybe? Or me bad citizen for think that?

Panel 6: Listen, man—What part of "Democracy Freedom Stay the Course Terror Terror" don't you understand?

Panel 7: I know. I feel bad. It's almost like the more syllables a word has, the more cracks there are for reality to seep through.

*April 16, 2004**

Panel 8: I loved it when the reporter was basically like, "Just who the hell exactly *are* we turning sovereignty over to on June 30th? Space Ghost?" And Bush said, "Fuck, I don't know— go ask Lakhdar Brahimi."

Panel 9: And everyone in America was like, "WHO THE FUCK IS LAKHDAR BRAHIMI? Can he balance the budget, too?"

Panel 10: You know the last country Brahimi saved? It's called "Afghanistan." I dare you to go live there.

April 16, 2004

April 16, 2004 (Apologies to B. Breathed)

April 16, 2004

April 23, 2004

Panel 1: Remind me why some people think Bush is tough? Because he walks around with his arms sticking out from his sides like an inflatable man? "You know how we do things in Crawford, Texas? When we have to answer tough questions, we get our Vice President to come along so he can *hold our hand like a goddamn baby.*"

Panel 2: Seriously, though? I would've asked Richard Perle to hold my hand. His hands look *so* soft.

Panel 3: That's because he's never had to wring them together, *because he's never been wrong.*

Panel 4: Hey—is Crawford, Texas secretly the touchy-feely capital of the world? If I ask a Crawford mechanic why he let my engine get fucked up, will the other guys in the garage be sitting there holding his hands the whole time?

April 29, 2004

Panel 1: First we threaten to deny Afghans humanitarian aid, then we torture Iraqi prisoners. These people were kind enough to let us *invade*—why treat 'em in such a totally half-assed way?

Panel 2: Hey, man. "Totally half-assed" is still much, much better than "totally Taliban'ed" or "totally Saddam'ed."

Panel 3: Well, *yeah.* But, dude, we're the goddamn *United States of America!* We have a flag on the moon, yet I'm supposed to be impressed we're doing a better job than *Saddam Hussein*? You sure we can't set the bar a little higher? Hell—the way things are going, I wouldn't be surprised if Iraq was better off being run by a fuckin' ATM machine and the cast of *Friends.*

Panel 4: Wait a minute. . . . "Totally half-assed" makes no sense.

Neither does "Donald Rumsfeld, Secretary of Defense." Get over it.

May 10, 2004

Panel 1: What rots first on a fish? The body or the head?

Panel 2: You know, when a fish gets rotten enough, you can't even *tell* the body from the head.

Panel 3: *Jesus!* My eyes are watering and I don't even *live* over there.

May 13, 2004

May 15, 2004

May 15, 2004

May 15, 2004

Strip 1:

Come on, June 30th! Come on, baby! Almost there!

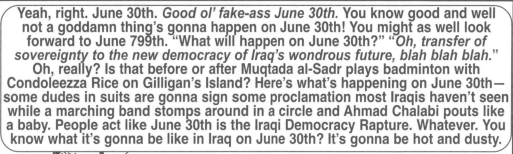

Yeah, right. June 30th. *Good ol' fake-ass June 30th.* You know good and well not a goddamn thing's gonna happen on June 30th! You might as well look forward to June 799th. "What will happen on June 30th?" "*Oh, transfer of sovereignty to the new democracy of Iraq's wondrous future, blah blah blah.*" Oh, really? Is that before or after Muqtada al-Sadr plays badminton with Condoleezza Rice on Gilligan's Island? Here's what's happening on June 30th— some dudes in suits are gonna sign some proclamation most Iraqis haven't seen while a marching band stomps around in a circle and Ahmad Chalabi pouts like a baby. People act like June 30th is the Iraqi Democracy Rapture. Whatever. You know what it's gonna be like in Iraq on June 30th? It's gonna be hot and dusty.

Maybe. But July 1st is gonna be AWESOME!

May 15, 2004

Strip 2:

Did you hear what Undersecretary of Defense Douglas Feith calls the State Department? "*The Department of Nice.*" Ouch.

Yeah. . . stupid *nice people.* Thank God they aren't in control of Iraq. What a disaster *that* would have been! Douglas Feith is the fucking stupidest guy on the face of the earth.

The more I learn, the more I'm relieved we entrusted postwar Iraq to the *Department of Mean.* Mean gets to the places Nice just can't reach!

Word—places like "*Undermining-our-moral-authority-ville.*" Thank you, Douglas Feith: The fucking stupidest guy on the face of the earth.

Hey! Enough with calling Douglas Feith the fucking stupidest guy on the face of the earth! We're fighting a war on terrorism, and you naive leftists are undermining it!

Actually, I didn't say Douglas Feith was the fucking stupidest guy on the face of the earth. Tommy Franks did. [Cough] *Naive leftist.*

Confidential to "T.F.": Would you be willing to write "Get Your War On" while I'm on vacation?

May 24, 2004

Strip 3:

You know what thought woke me up at three in the morning last night? Rumsfeld, Feith, and Perle are actually *more incompetent than they are evil.* How the hell is that possible?

You know what I realized? All these guys you see on TV, speaking about Iraq and sovereignty and June 30th and whatnot? *None of them has any fucking idea what they're talking about.* I listened to those blowhards for over a year and I didn't learn A SINGLE GODDAMN CORRECT THING. They talk out of their asses so much *their cushions are probably deaf.* I'd learn more about the future of Iraq if I read a Golden Book Encyclopedia upside-down in the dark.

Ooh—if you do that, will you look up the entry for "ignore?" I want to know if it still has that picture of Sudan.

May 27, 2004

Did you read that article in yesterday's *New York Times*? Explaining how it bravely chose to believe in Iraqi intelligence when others didn't have the courage to dream?

Brave, brave, *New York Times*! Now that everyone on earth knows *Ahmad Chalabi is Iraq's answer to fuckin' FAGIN,* you're looking for closure. Mmm. You know what a wise man once said: *"Fool me once, shame on— shame on you. . . you fool me, you can't get fooled again."* By the way, that's the mother-fucker WHOSE WAR YOU HELPED WAGE.

What's your problem? Isn't birdcage liner *supposed* to be absorbent?

May 27, 2004

Fuck a mild-mannered apology on Page 10. The only honest way for the *New York Times* to deal with this shit would have been to run a big-ass banner headline that says, "WHY THE HELL ARE YOU STILL READING US? DOES JUDITH MILLER HAVE TO KILL YOU HERSELF?"

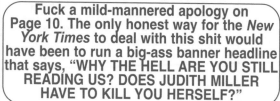

What about, "All the news that's fit to print, if by '*fit to print*' you mean '*that's actually un-fact-checkable horseshit pulled out of some con-man's ass and solemnly regurgitated on the front page, just so we could keep sitting at the tough guys table*'?"

And you know what's most embarrassing for the *Times*? They forgot to charge Chalabi a promotional fee.

May 27, 2004

Something really put things in perspective for me today. Kanan Makiya said he had a feeling of fore-boding about Iraq. He said postwar planning was a total failure. If he's feeling nervous, we're fucked.

I know. He was one of the few people whose pro-war arguments didn't make my retinas detach from my eyes rolling up in the back of my head. And now even *he* feels let down? What's next—our fuckin' *missiles* start feeling sad?

Poor guy. Sometimes you're so happy to finally get invited to the prom, you don't care who'll be breathing down your neck when the lights go out.

May 27, 2004

May 27, 2004

May 27, 2004

June 3, 2004*

June 28, 2004

June 28, 2004

June 28, 2004

June 28, 2004

June 28, 2004

WHY CAN'T I GET AWAY WITH FUCKING UP *GET YOUR WAR ON* LIKE DONALD RUMSFELD GETS AWAY WITH FUCKING UP WARS?

June 28, 2004

June 28, 2004

July 6, 2004

July 6, 2004

People who complain about the botched occupation seem to have forgotten one thing— *Donald Rumsfeld's military push towards Baghdad was brilliant.*

Yeah, right. Maybe I missed something, but wasn't the "military push" basically just us driving through the desert? That's "brilliant?" *Driving in a straight line to get somewhere?* And as far as defeating Saddam's army. . . look, no disrespect, but the goddamn *NBA* could have defeated Saddam's army. Big fuckin' deal—what was it, like a thousand malnourished motherfuckers in khakis shooting rifles from 1980? I bet the black-market price for white flags quadrupled in Iraq last spring. And our military thought *that* was the fight to win? Umm, *that wasn't the fight to win*, you strategic masterminds.

There's a new law at the Army War College: *Any fight with Ted Koppel riding in a tank is automatically not that important.*

July 6, 2004

Remember the Great Baghdad Power Vacuum of 2003? Is that what led to the Great Baghdad Disappointment Surplus of 2004?

Oh, come on. We owe the Iraqis *nothing.* We've given them their first taste of freedom in decades. We did a good thing, and they should thank us even if it, um, kills them.

Well, my question is always the same: When can I start blaming the guys in the sandals with all the guns pointed at them?

July 6, 2004

Look at me! I'm in *The Family Circus!*

July 6, 2004

You know what the CIA's motto is? *"I can't believe it's not intelligence!"*

You know what the White House's motto is? *"Waging a Never-Ending Global War On Terrorism means never having to say you're sorry. Because there's no time. Because we need to make up more crazy shit."*

You know what the FBI's motto is? *"The 'I' stands for 'I will never be fired.'"*

July 6, 2004

Will you tell me how the Argument For The War On Terrorism works?

If something good happens, it's *because* of our War On Terrorism. If something bad happens, it's in *spite* of it.

Hey, I like how that works! That's like church!

July 6, 2004

Oh—I almost forgot: Fuck you, you Islamic terrorists. Fuck you forever. You fuckin' insane backwards medieval farts. You're totally out of your fuckin' nasty-ass minds. Choppin' people's heads off. Fuckin' killing innocent people all the time. Blowing *yourselves* up. *Huh?* What the fuck is wrong with you? Sittin' around memorizing Koran verses and not even understanding what the fuck you're memorizing. Especially fuck that weird, woman-hating shit. Guess what? *Some people have breasts, vaginas and ovaries.* Oh my God, that's so crazy! Red alert—half your population are *not* sexually frustrated men in beards! And fuck how you don't trust science or movies or pop music. Are you fucking crazy? It's *pop music*, motherfuckers. We make it with synthesizers. DEAL WITH IT. You know what else? Women should be able to vote, and kids should learn math. Allah's OK with it, trust me. What's your logic? *"I know how we can stick it to Ariel Sharon—let's be the dumbest motherfuckers on earth. The more we don't know how to do calculus, the more we can defy Israel."* Nice. It's like you started a race to the end of the world, and you get off on running against America's worst elements. Great. Thanks a lot. *Chopping people's heads off.* What the fuck? Why do people take you seriously? Jesus Christ—it's like people are *deliberately* making it easy for me to hate them. Yeah, so fuck us—but fuck you more. And you know what? All this shit better be over before I have kids.

July 6, 2004

July 6, 2004

July 6, 2004

August 11, 2004

Columbus, Ohio, Fall 2004

Who are you gonna vote for on November 2nd?

It's tough, you know? I like that John Kerry served in the Korean(?) War. On the other hand, George Bush *is* the president, so I'd feel kind of funny voting against him.

Kabul, Afghanistan, Fall 2004

Who are you gonna vote for on October 9th?

It's tough, you know? Abdul Rashid Dostum has that whole *"I'm a warlord with just the tiniest lil' bit of blood on my hands"* appeal. On the other hand, Hamid Karzai has that whole *"Obi-Wan Kenobi in Prada"* American-puppet appeal.

Darfur, Sudan, Fall 2004

It's tough, you know?

August 13, 2004

I have to say, I'm impressed with how objective the press has been about this Swift boat issue. They're really giving me the space I need to make up my own mind. Does it help that I'm a stupid fuck?

That reminds me: How do you convince a Washington journalist that you're not slapping him in the face?

I don't know. How?

Tell him you're not.

August 23, 2004

You know when I realized it was important to get to the bottom of whether John Kerry threw his medals over the bow of his Swift b—*ahh fuck, who am I kidding?* I can't even keep track of what I'm supposed to give a fuck about, it's so goddamn retarded.

Come on, focus! Mekong Delta! Explosions, yes. . . *but how many?* Bronze star?!? Texas Guard National Air—

You know, there was a time when I would've been sad to hear that OVER A MILLION MORE AMERICANS ARE NOW LIVING IN POVERTY. But now my reaction is, "Good! *I hope it's all those Swift-boat-givin'-a-fuck idiots.*"

August 26, 2004

Umm. .. guess what every-body? I don't give a fuck about the Vietnam War. Fuck it. Why act like it's interesting to me? Hell, I don't even remember it.

I don't give a damn if you were a war hero, or a war criminal. Just shut the fuck up about it, OK? We've got, like, three wars going on right now IN THE PRESENT. I don't have *time* to give a fuck about Vietnam. You killed a bunch of Vietcong? Good for you. You sat on your ass and got drunk in Texas? Great. I really couldn't give a fuck. You had "other priorities?" Fine. *Get me some health insurance, you dumb motherfuckers.*

HEALTH INSURANCE? How am I supposed to read a newspaper article about *that?* You think I want to look at some *chart?*

August 26, 2004

Anyway, yeah, the Swift boat stuff is fun. So where's the real campaign? How do I get to see the real campaign?

This *is* the real campaign. This is it.

Wait a minute—you mean this is the real campaign even for the *grown-ups*???

August 26, 2004

What are stem cells? Two months ago I had never heard of them, but now politicians can't shut up about them. *Stem cells?* That's like, the most scientific thing a candidate has ever mentioned.

Why can't we have a national debate about something scientific that *I* like? *Endoplasmic reticulum in the mother-fuckin' house!!!*

If Bush is gonna keep arguing against science, why not go all the way and argue against *gravity?* I bet he could convince some of his supporters they were floating.

August 26, 2004

August 29, 2004

August 29, 2004

August 31, 2004

Panel 1: Hold up—Now Bush is saying we'll NEVER WIN the War on Terrorism? Who elected *him* Noam Chomsky?

Panel 2: I can't believe he said that. What the hell? I mean dude, sure—*you completely screwed up the Iraq war*. But it's OK; someone will fix it for you! Don't give up on us now!

Panel 3: It's like if someone strikes out at bat, and then turns around and predicts *nobody will ever be able to win a baseball game again*. Umm, actually, it's just that *you* will never be able to win a baseball game. Because you totally suck at baseball.

September 1, 2004

Panel 4: So as long as we'll never win the War on Terrorism, can we please stop fighting it? Or at least take a few months off?

Panel 5: But if we stopped fighting the War on Terrorism, what would Condoleezza Rice do all day?

Panel 6: Yeah—I'm so sure Condoleezza Rice *does something* all day!

September 1, 2004

Panel 7: You know, it almost makes me want to vote for Bush. Because what if he totally just cancels the War on Terrorism? What if he's like, "Fuck it—it's not like we're gonna *win* this shit. Let's do something fun with the money. Who wants a pony?"

Panel 8: If we stopped fighting the War on Terrorism, who would be responsible for taking Richard Perle seriously? The Tooth Fairy?

Panel 9: If we stopped fighting the War on Terrorism, it would free up more time for all of us to fight the REALLY important war: The *Vietnam* War.

September 1, 2004

Panel 1 (Row 1): You know what was the MOST AWESOME part of Schwarzenegger's speech? When he said Republicans would "TERMINATE" terrorism! Being eleven years old ROCKS!

Panel 2 (Row 1): And so, here we are—*I'm the only person who still takes the War on Terrorism seriously.* Who said irony was dead?

Panel 3 (Row 1): Or what about when he said people who are skeptical about the economy were "GIRLIE-MEN?" Ha. Who knew Schwarzenneger wrote his speech fifteen years ago? *That's* ambition.

September 1, 2004

Panel 1 (Row 2): The coolest thing about another four years of Bush would be the unveiling of the "Ownership Society!" Doesn't that sound bad-ass? You get to be in charge of your own Social Security!

Panel 2 (Row 2): Are you kidding me? *What the fuck would I want to be in charge of my Social Security for?* That's not my job. I don't know how to do that shit! And in case Bush is wondering, I don't want to have to deliver my own mail, either.

Panel 3 (Row 2): But it's the "Ownership Society." You will own part of society!

Panel 4 (Row 2): *Why do I gotta OWN EVERYTHING all of a sudden???*

September 1, 2004

Panel 1 (Row 3): In the Ownership Society, you get to buy stocks and make up your own medical plans! You get to be, like, your own personal government. *I'm gonna issue a coin with my face on it!*

Panel 2 (Row 3): I will agree to participate in the Ownership Society if white collar crime becomes a capital offense. Like, if motherfuckers get *hung*.

Panel 3 (Row 3): It's funny—when I first heard Bush mention the new Ownership Society, I thought he was talking about Iraq. I was like, "Dude, don't just come right out and *say* it!"

September 1, 2004

Oh, my God! Have you read the latest news about the war in . . . *Vietnam*?

(*Sigh*) The Vietnam War. I love that this election is gonna be decided on how people acted during the fucking *Vietnam War*. Like there's not enough wars going on RIGHT NOW to keep us interested. Fuck the Vietnam War. I'm not worried about the fuckin' *Viet Cong* flying airplanes into buildings, you idiots! Unless someone can convince me that Osama bin Laden is currently hiding out in the Mekong Delta thirty-five years ago, I don't want to hear another peep about the stupid goddamn Vietnam War.

But if you'd just listen to the Swift Boat Veterans for Tru—

Oh, yeah! I totally forgot to listen to the Swift Boat Jackasses for Horseshit! *No wonder I can still count to ten and tie my own shoes!* I love books that actually make you MORE STUPID with each page. *How do you tell how many times someone has read "Unfit for Command"? Easy— just count how many fingers they've got stuck up their nose!*

September 15, 2004

If Iraq descends into a civil war, will Bush get to count it as one of his?

In a civil war, who gets naming rights? Will the Kurds and Sunnis have different names for it? I'm probably gonna root for the Kurds, so I guess I'll go with their name.

The only fair thing would be to let Paul Wolfowitz name it. After all, it's his baby whether he owns up to it or not.

September 20, 2004

So the best-case scenario for Iraqis involves "tenuous security"? What kind of dipshit best-case scenario is that? "Tenuous" is a *worst-case scenario* word. Hell, I don't want to hear "tenuous" when I'm talking about a *barbecue*, let alone a country full of angry motherfuckers I can't understand! That's like saying, "Don't worry. . . the bullets in this gun are just *tenuous*." Fuck that! I'm not into tenuous. *Tenuous isn't cutting it for me.*

Oh, come on—if Iraqis had something better than tenuous security, how could they be sure they were still living in Iraq? We're probably just being culturally sensitive.

Sure, cultural sensitivity is important. Isn't that why we capped the corporate tax rate in Iraq at 15%?

September 20, 2004

Panel 1: I like President Bush's optimism about Iraq. I wish he'd go over there and walk the streets and share it with Iraqis personally. Seems kind of silly to waste it all behind a podium.

Panel 2: But there's a reason for his optimism: We handed out more free soccer balls in Baghdad!

Panel 3: Great. And what the fuck are we supposed to do when some insurgent figures out how to kill people using soccer balls?

September 20, 2004

Panel 4: Is Toby Keith gonna sing a song about US military cutting off the water and electricity in Tall Afar? Has he ever crossed over to the Rhythm & Possible War Crimes chart?

Panel 5: Maybe the Army thought it'd be cool if Iraqis thirsted for something other than freedom for a few days.

Panel 6: Yeah. There's nothing like literal thirst to put metaphorical thirst in perspective.

September 20, 2004

Panel 7: The only thing that got Tall Afar's citizens through the days of being denied electricity and running water was the inspiration of that sweet 15% corporate tax rate! *"Mommy, I'm gonna improve my market capitalization as soon as this parasite leaves my body!"*

Panel 8: *"Ooh, Mommy, you know the only thing worse than having a marginal tax rate above 15%? Having dehydration-related diarrhea in the dark!"*

Panel 9: How long would Heritage Foundation pundits let *their* children go without running water, if the reward was a flat 15% tax rate? I bet they'd put those Iraqi parents to shame.

September 20, 2004

I love how the only sure thing in Iraq is a 15% corporate tax rate. . . *and that the corporate tax rate is actually lower than the probability of all-out CIVIL WAR.* Freedom is almost *too much* on the march.

I wonder if Bush would be willing to peg the Iraqi corporate tax rate to the probability of delaying a civil war until after the US election. I wonder where he'd draw the line? *Do I hear fifty-one per cent?*

The way Bush is acting so nonchalant, I wouldn't be surprised if he thought civil wars *only* occur in the United States in the 1860s. "Thank God nobody named *Jefferson Davis* lives in Iraq, huh Don? Then we might have a problem!"

September 20, 2004

Who cares if the White House suppressed evidence about Saddam Hussein's aluminum tubes? Who cares if they can't actually process uranium? They're still made out of *aluminum*. I think we should go to war over anything that ends in *-um*.

Condoleezza Rice told me you can process uranium with empty Mountain Dew cans— if you're *evil* enough.

If Saddam Hussein didn't have all those tubes, do you think the White House would have insisted that you can process uranium with tacky palaces and a moustache?

October 4, 2004

It's official: Hamid Karzai was finally elected president of Afghanistan! I *told* you freedom was on the march.

I wish *I* could be elected president of a big pile of rubble!

You see, that's how bad-ass freedom and democracy are—they don't sit around waiting until there's actually something to *govern* in Afghanistan. They just jump onstage and start changing peoples' lives! (By the way, does Afghanistan know I'm never going to think about it again?)

October 11, 2004

A PLEDGE TO THOSE WHO HAVEN'T DECIDED WHO TO VOTE FOR
BUT ARE SURE THEY HATE THIS COMIC.   JUST IN CASE IT TIPS THE BALANCE.

> *If John Kerry wins the election,*
> *I will stop making "Get Your War On."*
> *You'll never have to read it again.*

PLEASE VOTE NOVEMBER 2nd !

October 12, 2004

October 18, 2004

October 25, 2004

Strip 1:

I guess when Rumsfeld said he wanted to transform the American military, he meant "*transform it into a bunch of blown-up people.*"

You know how President Bush slams critics of Operation Iraqi Freedom for "second-guessing our commanders in the field during a time of war?" Umm... Consider our commanders in the field during a time of war officially second-guessed. In fact, I'd be happy to third-, fourth-, and *fifth*-fuckin'-guess 'em—that is, of course, if THEY'RE NOT TOO BUSY ALLOWING IRAQI INSURGENTS TO CARRY OFF 380 TONS OF EXPLOSIVES.

Sure, you laugh now—but what about when Saddam Hussein caused 9/11?

October 25, 2004

Strip 2:

Do you think Mohamed ElBaradei is currently running around with 380 tons of Schadenfreude?

The worst thing about working at the IAEA is that nobody can hear you say "I told you so." On account of all the explosions.

God, wouldn't it be ironic if the Iraq war actually somehow *increased* terrorism? Who could have foreseen such irony? Maybe ninety percent of the world or something?

October 25, 2004

Strip 3:

When I first heard about the looted weapons stockpiles, I was like "Damn— that's a ton of explosives!" And then I said it again three hundred and seventy-nine times, to be accurate.

I wouldn't have thought there was 380 tons of *anything* in Iraq, except maybe sand.

If Iraqi insurgents steal more tons of explosives than we pull down of Saddam Hussein statues, do they win?

October 25, 2004

October 25, 2004

ELECTION 2004: *The People Have Spoken*

November 8, 2004

November 15, 2004

Which of these things is **NOT LIKE** the others?

A.

B.

C.

D.

ANSWER: **D.** (A sandwich isn't a tool.)

November 16, 2004

November 22, 2004

November 29, 2004

Man, you know who they need to fire? Kofi Annan, man. He's incompetent! Something UN oil-for-food something something!

Hell, I'm in favor of firing Kofi Annan. I'm in favor of firing the whole goddamn UN. I'm in favor of firing anyone who had anything to do with Iraq over the last thirty years. Fire anyone who wrote about it. Fire anyone who read about it. Fuck it—fire the guy who sweeps the floor at National Geographic. There's not enough people on Earth to fire, to make it up to Iraq.

No, just fire Kofi Annan. Donald Rumsfeld will make it up to Iraq by himself.

December 6, 2004

I don't give a damn about "mandates" and "political capital"—George W. Bush is still an amoral, cynical son of a bitch who completely screwed up Iraq. And you Red Staters who voted for him should prepare to have your minds blown when my **POLITICAL WEDDING BAND** shows up at your reception!

This solo symbolizes the media's *pounding the war drum* for Bush in the run-up to the Iraq war! Enjoy ...

I dedicate my performance of "Brown Eyed Girl" to the innocent victims of the Fallujah assault! Let's see some people on the dance floor!

Ladies and gentlemen, it's a magical day for Matt and Tina—*but not for the 15,000 Iraqi civilians we've fuckin' KILLED in the past two years*! Hokeypokey, anyone?

Well, in *spite* of the band, this is still the happiest day of my life.

Yeah. I wish my brother was here to see it.

December 8, 2004

God bless **SWEET LITTLE BABY** Donald Rumsfeld, the Prince of Peace

"What is this then that is written, The stone which the builders rejected, the same is become the head of the corner?

Whosoever shall fall upon that stone shall be broken;

but on whomsoever it shall fall, it will grind him to powder." (Luke 20:17-18)

December 13, 2004

And what do *you* want for Christmas, my grumpy little friend?

What do I want for Christmas? I want to be wrong. I want to be totally wrong about everything. And I mean *embarrassingly* wrong. I want Iraq to be a flourishing, humane, free-market democracy this time next year, and to actually turn to me and say, "In your *face*, cynical New York man! Your visionary president sowed the seeds of democracy in me while you stood around and belly-ached!" And then I'll be like, "Damn, I guess I never really *did* have any idea what the fuck I was moaning about, huh? My bad, Mr. President."

Doesn't it get old, wishing for the same thing every Christmas?

December 19, 2004

BIONIC ABU GHRAIB MAN

Bad news, guys—Bionic Abu Ghraib Man is on the loose! *And there's no telling what he'll do!*

You say that like it's a *bad* thing!

REGULAR ABU GHRAIB MAN!!! Who let you in here?

Not me, boss! Heck, I had forgotten about him.

Yeah! Who wants to remember a guy who looks like a *stalagmite*?

December 20, 2004

What do we know about the origin of Bionic Abu Ghraib Man?

Not much, sir— He's a mystery. (*Sigh.*) *If only that super-genius George Tenet was still around to explain everything. . .*

I bet you could trace Bionic Abu Ghraib Man's origin to the morning after November 2, 2004.

REGULAR ABU GHRAIB MAN!!! This is no time for moralizing! Get down off your soap box!

But if I get down off my box, they'll electrocute my PENIS!

December 20, 2004

"Like Regular Abu Ghraib Man, Bionic Abu Ghraib Man was spawned in a midnight legal laboratory by Alberto Gonzales."

"And like Regular Abu Ghraib Man, Bionic Abu Ghraib Man has a bunch of wires connected to his hands."

"However, we believe Bionic Abu Ghraib Man has figured out how to *harness the energy of those wires* for his own nihilistic ends!"

December 20, 2004

Killer! I totally just jumped over that weird black thing!

This sucks!

Nobody takes me seriously. I wish Bionic Abu Ghraib Man was here!

Oh my God! It's Bionic Abu Ghraib Man! **HOLY SHIT, HE LOOKS AMAZING**

He's even more mechanical and intimidating than I imagined! *I wonder if he has special powers?*

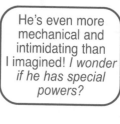

December 20, 2004

NOW YOU KNOW

Oh Jesus! He's headed right at us!

Literally or metaphorically? LITERALLY OR METAPHORICALLY? *I can't turn my head!*

December 20, 2004

PRACTICE THE GUITAR? What's the point? Some gigantic tsunami will just come along and kill you and 225,000 other innocent people.

You need to replace your bass strings, but then again— **WHY BOTHER?** It's not like some stupid *bass strings* will stop the incredible **KILLIN' FEVER** that's sweeping the world.

Boo-hoo! Iraqi civilian casualties, illegal war, Halliburton, blah blah blah. **TELL IT TO THE TSUNAMI.**

WOULDN'T IT BE GREAT if this was your life? Just rockin' out with your buds and never leaving the garage to learn how many more people have died?

January 3, 2005

The Iraqi elections are almost here! Freedom is almost done marching. Man, I'd hate to see Freedom's bunions at this point.

I bet when Freedom finally unlaces its boots, some people will *keel over* at the odor.

Not Bush. He won't keel over. He'll *swoon.*

January 17, 2005*

Oh, my God! Social Security is in a CRISIS!!! And the only way out is to let me invest my payments in Powerball tickets—NOW!!!

Once President Bush privatizes Social Security, will babies have to pay for their Social Security numbers?

I bet rich people will pay extra for vanity Social Security numbers. Like, Bill O'Reilly could get "LUV-2-PH0N3."

January 19, 2005

How can you not love our new Secretary of State? Have you ever heard her **PLAY THE PIANO?** Seriously, dude, she's *really good* at playing the piano. Her interpretation of Rachmaninov's Sonata No. 1 really brings out the piece's lack of diplomacy.

And when she performed the **BRAHMS VIOLIN SONATA NO. 3** with Yo Yo Ma, you truly *believed* Brahms's crap about Iraq's non-existent WMDs by the last movement. Brilliant.

But I think her wonderful talent is at its best when applied to Chopin's later works. She draws out his whimsical melodies without over-emphasizing the subharmonics of dead people and billions of dollars flushed down the fucking toilet.

January 24, 2005

Hey buddy! What did you think of those elections in Iraq? I bet they blew your liberal mind! Ha ha! *YOU WERE WRONG! BUSH WAS RIGHT! YOU WERE WRONG! BUSH WAS RIGHT! Freedom freedom, fight fight fight!!!*

Yeah, I was wrong. Especially when I told everyone that Iraqis hate freedom and enjoyed living under Saddam Hussein. *I'm so embarrassed you remember how I always used to say that.*

I can't tell if you're being sarcastic or not, so I'm just going to continue chanting until Jesus tells me to forget about Iraq.

January 31, 2005

If the Iraqi elections taught me anything, it's that **MEN WHO DREAM BIG** need to be patient. There will always be skeptics, doubters and snarky political cartoonists who assume anti-democratic forces will win every time. Well, **NOT THIS TIME.**

And I have to admit, even though this leader gives me the creeps, he stood firm against **THOSE WHO DIDN'T WANT A REAL DEMOCRATIC PROCESS** in Iraq. He will be remembered as a true friend of the Iraqi people. I won't.

So thank you, **GRAND AYATOLLAH ALI AL-SISTANI.** *You can now tell the Baathist playa-haters AND the White House to step off your jammy!*

Don't know who Sistani is? Congratulations: You are now officially **TOO STUPID** to talk about Iraq. Shut the fuck up.

February 2, 2005

I wonder if President Bush is having fun "mending fences" in Europe? Like he's ever mended anything in his life.

Just when I'm afraid I only have enough hate for *one* world leader, I remember who's running France, Germany, Italy and Russia. It's like a buffet of assholes: *"I can't believe I hate the whole thing!"*

I just hope Bush can survive the press conferences. Did he remember to pack a softball-lobbing male prostitute with a fake name?

February 21, 2005

I'm gonna be so pissed if Iran is secretly developing nuclear weapons. Do you know how many more weird-ass foreign names we'll have to remember? For, like, six months?

It's not that bad. Just forget one Iraqi player's name for each Iranian player's name: Goodbye, Adnan Pachachi! Hellooo, Mohammed Reza Khatami!

Wait a minute—what do I do with Ahmed Chalabi's name? Just move it from one column to the other?

February 28, 2005

You know what I just realized? I bet every so often those ROLLING STONE readers who are currently deployed in Iraq and Afghanistan get tired of reading **OBNOXIOUS CRITICISM** about their mission and their commander in chief. So this issue, we're gonna take a little break: It's **NCAA BASKETBALL** time.

What happened to the Jayhawks? They're tanking like the Fallujah real-estate market.

As long as Duke's hurting, who cares? My team can be 0 and 24, as long as Duke is -1 and 23. I'm surprised their uniforms don't have little collars to turn up like James Spader in a John Hughes movie.

Ah, yes. Good ol' Mike Krzyzewski— the Henry Kissinger of men's basketball.

March 1, 2005

March 14, 2005

March 25, 2005

March 25, 2005

First of all, let me a give a shout to all my fellow feeding tubes out there. I hope you guys are making a positive difference in someone's life—*unlike me.*

I've been inside Terri Schiavo for fifteen years and it hasn't done SHIT. *This is professionally humiliating to me as a feeding tube.* I might as well be a goddamn *shoelace* for all the good I'm doing. Let me go to an Iraqi hospital and blow their minds, that a nice piece of medical equipment actually decided to show up for once. See, that would make me feel good: *To feed people who actually know that they are hungry.*

Instead, they got me wrapped up in all this bullshit! "Culture of Life?" You're gonna start legislating based on phrases stolen from herbal tea packaging? Why not "Sleepytime Lemon Traditions?" Fuckin' hold midnight congressional sessions about *that,* you dumb fucks! Seriously—you better hope you never see me in Terri again, unless you want your stillbirths subpoenaed someday.

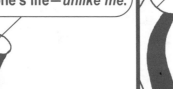

March 25, 2005*

My wife and I made our living wills last night. Mine says that if I fall into a persistent vegetative state, and Tom DeLay comes within a hundred miles of me, *I am to turn into a zombie and rip his fucking head off.* They can't prosecute the undead for manslaughter, can they?

Well, technically, in your case the charge wouldn't be manslaughter. It'd be insecticide.

When you think about it, zombies would make a compelling counter-argument to the Culture of Life.

March 25, 2005

If pulling out a feeding tube after fifteen years is *starving someone to death,* pulling up a zipper is *castration.*

Pull the tube out. And don't stop pulling 'til you've pulled the troops out. Leave the Iraqis a blank check and all the chlorinated water they can handle. Leave the Floridians a gift certificate to Applebee's and a goodbye note. It's time to amputate. *Before the bullshit spreads from Florida to America's torso.*

I can just hear Rhode Island screaming: "Help! We're being attacked by the Culture of Life! Send zombies!"

March 25, 2005

Hamid Karzai picked an opportunistic warlord with blood on his hands to be the equivalent of his vice-president.

Are you *insane*? What the hell does Afghanistan have to do with the feeding tube?

Well, most people think Rashid Dostum is going to ease the way for the long-planned "feeding tube" running from Turkmenistan to Pakistan.

Ah, so! *Feeding tube!*

March 25, 2005

You didn't listen to Bush's speech at the National Defense University, did you? Some Sun Tzu wannabe at work had it on, and I stuffed so much cotton in my ears I WEPT TAMPONS.

Dude, I *liked* the speech! I'm a fan of Bush's words about democracy in the Middle East. I only wish that once they left his mouth, they'd turn around in midair and join together to form a *magical word-fist* and knock him upside the head until he took 'em seriously.

Sounds like they're finally taking 'em seriously in Lebanon . . .

Oh, "*finally,*" huh? Listen to Dr. Encyclopedia Lebanonnica over here!

Also: *feeding tube*

March 25, 2005

Did you see the president's mommy out there trying to help sell his Social Security piratization scheme?

I gotta say, I was a little disappointed with that shit. *You're the president, dude!* You still call on your *mom* when you're in hot water? You couldn't get Aquaman or Green Lantern or some other tough motherfucker? Dude, your *mom?*

Here's a hint: Any time someone arguing for privatizing Social Security is wearing a pearl necklace worth more than her audience's total assets, keep some grains of salt handy. Like, a *Cape Hatteras* of salt.

March 28, 2005

The State Department has published "Patterns of Global Terrorism," a summary of international terror attacks, every year since 1985. **BUT NOT THIS YEAR.** Why not? *Hmm.* Could it have anything to do with the fact that 2004 had **MORE INTERNATIONAL TERROR ATTACKS** *than any year since 1985?* Or has Condoleezza Rice just **USED UP HER PHOTOCOPYING BUDGET FOR 2005?**

I'm telling you, man— we're winning the Global War on Terrorism! Terrorists are straight-up runnin' out of terror!

Are you sure? Have you checked this year's "Patterns of Global Terrorism?"

Dude, didn't you hear? There were so few attacks last year, *the report was the size of a single molecule.* That's why nobody has seen it!

March 28, 2005

Seriously, don't get your panties in a bunch—lots of 2004's terror attacks were in Kashmir. We're winning the War on Terrorism everywhere else.

Oh, it's just *Kashmir* that's blowing up? What a relief. I was worried about terror attacks in *volatile* regions of the world—not in regions angrily contested by nuclear rivals struggling against anti-government religious fundamentalists. *Yawn.*

Don't forget ". . .and that we're about to start selling a lot of F-16s to!"

March 28, 2005

Hooray! **ELECTIONS IN ZIMBABWE!** Ain't nothin' like a little democracy to put things right in a troubled land ...

How do you pronounce "Robert Mugabe?" When I curse a motherfucker, I like to pronounce his last name correctly.

Mugabe rhymes with "*Starving your citizens is a really fun hobby.*"

Ah! Does it rhyme with "*I love it when kids' bellies are distended and their knees and elbows are all knobby* "?

April 4, 2005

I had a great idea for a comic about the **PENTAGON'S POST-9/11 PROGRESS** in teaching Arabic skills to its military personnel. Unfortunately, I couldn't find a clip-art picture of a committee of retarded snails with **ONE THOUSAND THUMBS STUCK UP THEIR BUTTS** slowly backing away from a burning tower into a **BOTTOMLESS PIT OF MOLASSES.** We'll just have to make do . . .

The 9/11 attacks compelled the Department of Defense to commission a study "assessing language needs" in September. Of 2003. Or was that the *Turbo* Department of Defense?

My assessment is that one of their language needs is comprehending the vernacular English expression "Hurry the fuck up, you retards!"

And then, like a speeding bullet that is not so much *"speeding"* as it is *"imitating the charming entropy of a cumulus cloud on a lazy summer afternoon,"* last spring the Department of Defense finally ordered *its* agencies to "assess language needs." We'd be better off handing out Speak & Spells duct-taped to the Koran.

April 10, 2005

Hey, good news—the Department of Defense is getting serious about foreign-language training. It's gonna publish a "guidance for language program management" by July 2005! Hot damn! *I bet we'll know what al-Qaeda is saying by 2041!*

I already *know* what al-Qaeda is saying: "Damn, it sure takes infidels a long time to decide to learn Arabic. Let's learn Swahili and *really* fuck with 'em!"

You know, thanks to Rumsfeld, I bet the military has heard a *few* Arabic phrases enough to memorize 'em, like: *"Arjouk, la tughsubnee an ada'a isba'ee fee tizi wa al-hasuhu."**

* "Please don't make me stick my finger up my ass and lick it."

April 12, 2005

Remember when everyone's favorite answer to "Why are we going to war in Iraq?" was "Saddam Hussein gassed his own people"? It's true: In 1988, **THAT SICK FUCK GASSED AND KILLED** 5,000 innocent Kurds in the town of Halabja. **IF ANYONE HAD REASON TO BE EXCITED ABOUT THE AMERICAN INVASION,** it was the survivors. So we drove through the desert, pulled down some statues, and promised Iraqis we'd get to work rebuilding their infrastructure—you know, minor, unimportant shit like **ACCESS TO CLEAN DRINKING WATER.** Funny thing happened: We just canceled the water project in Halabja. Sweet. No clean drinking water for the survivors of Saddam Hussein's most brutal chemical weapons attack! **WOULDN'T WANT TO SPOIL THEM,** I guess. (By the way, the official State Department web page about the Halabja attack actually misspells the word "tragedy.")

Damn, he didn't leave us much room this week!

Seriously! I feel like I'm trapped under a truck. There's not even room for a punchline!

No punchline? That's a tradgedy!

April 18, 2005

I'll tell you one thing: If I had survived Saddam Hussein's worst chemical weapons attack, and then spent fifteen years drinking unsanitary water while I waited for America to invade; and then waited another two years *after* the invasion for the reconstruction project that would finally supply sanitary drinking water; and then found out that the project had been canceled and *nobody had bothered to tell me*—one thing I would *not* want would be a glass of unsanitary drinking water. Not even if it had the world's coolest bendy-straw in it.

I'm sorry—if the United States can't supply clean drinking water to the town of Halabja, the United States officially *can't do shit.*

Can't do or won't do?

April 18, 2005

Wow! Am I really talking to Thomas Friedman? THE Thomas Friedman?

Yes you are! And here's the exciting thing, Bob: Because THE WORLD IS FLAT, we're all actually closer than ever—for better *and* for worse. For instance, last week I was eating sushi with a Bengali venture capitalist, who couldn't wait to show me his new cell phone—

Whoa, hold up: Did you just say the world is *flat*? That's a counterintuitive statement. Have you gone plain ol' *crazy*, Thomas Friedman?

April 20, 2005

It's a *metaphor*, Bob—a picture I painted *using my words*. "Flatness" represents how we live in a new, flat world, where flatness has flattened bumpiness; where the next *"space race"* will actually be a gigantic *"most-flattest flat-off"*—

That makes no sense. The world's not flat. If the world was flat, I could just live at the corner farthest from al-Qaeda and relax, 'cause I'd be able to see them coming from a mile off.

Ahh. *Skeptical.* You're not wearing The Moustache of Understanding. Tell you what— I'll share mine. I'm going to transmit it to you via my UNCANNY OPTIMISM.

April 20, 2005

April 20, 2005

AUSTIN, TEXAS — The state House tentatively approved legislation that would **PROHIBIT HOMOSEXUALS AND BISEXUALS FROM BECOMING FOSTER PARENTS** .... "*It is our responsibility to make sure that we protect our most vulnerable children, and I don't think we are doing that if we allow a foster parent that is homosexual or bisexual,*" said Rep. Robert Talton, a Republican, who introduced the amendment. (The Associated Press, 4/20/05)

FUCK THE CARTOON THIS WEEK. My wife used to be a therapist for teens in foster-care group homes. These were kids who had suffered abandonment, abuse and neglect. They were often profoundly lonely. I don't mean lonely like, "Oh, none of my friends can hang out today—shucks, I'm so lonely."

I mean profoundly lonely.

Night after night, my wife would come home and tell me what profoundly lonely children do: Girls snuck out to meet "boyfriends," money stashed in their vaginas in case they got jumped. Boys just shut down, too depressed to bathe. The group homes were sad places, and kids lived in them for years, waiting to be placed with foster parents.

Of course, many of them were never placed.

So now we have to read about Robert Talton, a Republican member of the Texas House of Representatives, who wants to make it illegal for gay Americans to give of themselves as foster parents. *Illegal.*

It must be nice, to be some piece of shit in a suit and tie who gets to make up laws in Texas.

April 24, 2005

April 25, 2005

May 2, 2005

May 9, 2005

Federal judges are **A MORE SERIOUS THREAT TO AMERICA** than Al Qaeda and the Sept. 11th terrorists, the Rev. Pat Robertson claimed yesterday. . . . Confronted by [George] Stephanopoulos on his claims that an out-of-control judiciary is the worst threat America has faced in 400 years—**WORSE THAN NAZI GERMANY, JAPAN AND THE CIVIL WAR**—Robertson didn't back down. (New York *Daily News*, 5/2/05)

So here's my offer: I'll spend a year in the company of *federal judges* if Pat Robertson will just spend a year in a Nazi concentration camp. No, wait—*I'll actually fly on a 747 with federal judges* if Pat Robertson will just please fly on a 747 with Islamic terrorists. No, wait—I've got it. I'll move to Pakistan and open a madrassah and *recruit the Islamic terrorists myself* and sneak 'em into the country and buy the box cutters and the Osama bin Laden books-on-tape or whatever so the fuckers can get all wet for jihad—all Pat Robertson has to do is show up, sit on the plane, and think about how scary federal judges are while his ass flies into a skyscraper. Heck, I'll even pay for his ticket.

Stop making fun! If you don't . . . *the federal judges will have won.*

May 9, 2005

What the fuck is going on in Uzbekistan, our steadfast ally in the War on Terror?

What, you don't like how the Uzbek government practices the delicate art of crowd control? You got a problem with babies' brains splattered all over the town square?

Meow! Don't cry over spilt brains! Those babies weren't really using 'em anyway!

Aw, it's cute li'l Uzbekikitty—the steadfast putty tat with good basing opportunities!

May 16, 2005

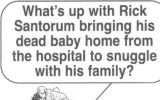

What's up with Rick Santorum bringing his dead baby home from the hospital to snuggle with his family?

CULTURE OF LIFE!!! *You got a problem with that?*

Right. . . But the baby was *dead*. I'm all in favor of bringing *living* babies home from the hospital. But why have your family cuddle a baby's corpse?

You don't understand the Culture of Life— it's *pro-cuddling-babies'- corpses*. Why do you think we invaded Iraq?

I thought I said NO DEAD BABY JOKES!

(BEAR-SYMPATHIZING CARTOONIST)

May 23, 2005

"A cable sent May 13 by the United States Embassy in Kabul to Secretary of State Condoleezza Rice asserted that [poppy] eradication efforts were slipping partly because, 'although President Karzai has been **WELL AWARE OF THE DIFFICULTY** in trying to implement an effective ground eradication program, he has been **UNWILLING TO ASSERT STRONG LEADERSHIP**. . . .' " (*New York Times*, 5/22/05)

Get out! You mean Hamid Karzai is actually *reluctant* to quash the one real moneymaking opportunity in all of Afghanistan? That doesn't surprise me—*and I'm a goddamn armadillo.*

What the fuck else are they gonna grow in Afghanistan? Broken Soviet airplanes?

You know, it's a shame junkies can't get high off old land mines.

May 23, 2005

So we all believe that the new oil pipeline from Azerbaijan to Turkey will "strengthen peace and security in the region," right? Because we're all totally fuckin' crazy, right?

Ilham Aliyev, President of Azerbaijan
His police recently beat the shit out of pro-democracy demonstrators. It's illegal to protest against him. *Pipeline time!*

The only way that pipeline will bring peace and security to the region is ~~caught within a hundred yard~~ ~~licked in the groin~~

We interrupt this (awesome) cartoon for a **TECHNICAL QUESTION:** Why is it that our allies in the Central Asian republics look **TOTALLY FIENDISH** when I convert their photos to black & white? Is Adobe Photoshop actually **A BETTER JUDGE OF CHARACTER** than President Bush?

May 30, 2005

Did we violate the Cuban trade embargo when we shipped Korans over to Guantanamo? Or are we defiling *Cuban* Korans?

This whole few-instances-of-Koran-defilement uproar is bullshit. At least we *gave 'em Korans*. You think if al-Qaeda captured you they'd provide you with a copy of *Foundation of Metaphysics of Morals* or whatever that shit is you read?

True. And I guess, since I believe *all* spiritual texts should be defiled, I can't be too picky. I just wish the hicks running Guantanamo had started with *Dianetics*.

June 6, 2005

🇬🇧 *It's The British Memo Invasion!!!* 🇬🇧

Ooh, I'm all atwitter about the British Memo Invasion! They're *ever* so fresh and exciting! Who's your favorite memo?

(*Giggle*) I have a crush on *Downing Street!* But there aren't many articles about him. (*Sigh*) I wish he wasn't so camera-shy. . .

At first I wondered why there weren't more screaming girls for this British Invasion. Then I remembered—the screaming girls are in Iraq.

June 13, 2005

June 20, 2005

July 4, 2005

*George W. Bush's view of Tony Blair at the G8 Summit.

July 4, 2005

Come on, can't you think of something funny to say about the London attacks? Something about how hard it must be for that two-bit, ghetto-ass, hook-handed Imam to applaud 'em?

I'm thinking, I'm thinking! Jesus, give me a minute to be *upset*, why don't you—

I know there's a joke here somewhere. It involves the phrases "Karl Rove" and "let the healing begin," but I can't figure out how to make it work.

July 7, 2005

Hello. I'm Elitist McLefty, the creator of "Get Your War On." I'm here at my drafting table. Yep—this is where I draw the comic you're reading!

I wanted to speak to you about the London bombings. Have you noticed that, somehow, everyone has been able to use the bombings to "prove" their arguments about foreign policy? It's miraculous. From assholes on Fox News saying the bombings prove we shouldn't care about African poverty, to anti-war activists saying the bombings prove we should withdraw from Iraq tomorrow.

What a bunch of baloney! The bombings prove one thing only: *Political cartoonists are underpaid.* That's the only goddamn thing the bombings prove. Look at my old drafting table—you think it's easy to draw the same person over and over on this lumpy-ass thing? *The bombings prove I need a raise so I can buy a new drafting table!* (And a pony.)

July 11, 2005

Jesus *Christ* is it humid! When people talked about the Karl Rove scandal heating up, I assumed it would be a *dry* heat. Instead I need a towel to dry my towel before I dry myself.

Karl Rove controls the amount of dampness in the air by modulating his soft, fleshy non-chin. When he is persecuted, the air grows moist with his anger. *Prepare thyself for the Great Enmoistening!*

Seriously, this is no fun. It's *really* goddamn humid. I'm not trying to make a satirical point— I'm just complaining. It is straight up, 100% just plain ol' too goddamn humid!

July 18, 2005

"In language both **SHARP AND SUBTLE,** Iraqi and international officials on Monday criticized the U.S.-led rebuilding effort for **MOVING TOO SLOWLY** to improve the lives of Iraqi citizens. . . . The criticism reflected a growing belief . . . that the Bush administration had **BUNGLED THE RECONSTRUCTION** by giving billions to private corporations to tackle major infrastructure projects." (*Los Angeles Times*, 7/19/05)

"Language both sharp and subtle"? Hmm . . . How do you say anything *subtle* about Bush's Iraq "reconstruction"? That's like saying something subtle about finding your dick in an anthill.

Allow me. I am the master of language most subtle. (*Ahem*) "*Just as the lotus flower's delicate fragrance drifts along the breeze at sunset's whimsy, so too does the Bush administration BUNGLE THE HOLY GODDAMN LIVING FUCK out of Iraq's reconstruction.*" You see, child, subtle language can soften criticism's sting, just as dawn's rosy mist can soften—

Enough with your dawn's rosy mist. When do we impeach these fuckers?

July 20, 2005

What's more complicated and boring—the *"Valerie Plame / Karl Rove / CIA identity leak"* thing or the *"Iraqi constitutional process / tenuous Sunni participation / people still getting blown up"* thing?

I can't follow either of 'em. It's August—any news story that can't be summarized in five strokes of a green crayon is beyond me.

Newspapers should have a policy for the summer months where, instead of actually trying to explain anything, they just dump a bucket of blood on your doorstep. And you can think about it or not.

July 25, 2005

So Bush's approval rating is around 44%. When I first saw that number, I kept looking for a decimal point. *How can there not be a decimal point in that approval rating? For the love of God, what does it TAKE???*

No decimal point yet. Check back in a year— I bet we'll see 4.4%.

I know America will be on the right track when it looks like Bush's approval ratings are pegged to interest rates. And I don't mean credit card interest rates—fuck 24.99%— I mean some *free checking account* interest rates.

August 1, 2005

August 5, 2005

August 15, 2005

August 15, 2005

"The Bush administration is **SIGNIFICANTLY LOWERING EXPECTATIONS** of what can be achieved in Iraq, recognizing that the United States will have to settle for far less progress than originally envisioned. . . . The United States no longer expects to see a model new democracy, a self-supporting oil industry or a society in which the majority of people are free from serious security or economic challenges. . . ." (The *Washington Post*, 8/14/05)

 Oh well. At least nobody got hurt!

 At least, nobody *I* know got hurt.

August 16, 2005

 Farewell, Gaza settlers! Thank you for reminding me that Jews can be crazy assholes, too.

 Have the settlers settled on where they'll settle next?

 I think this is when they all climb into their Battlestar Galactica ship and speed through the galaxy, all the way over to the West Bank.

August 22, 2005

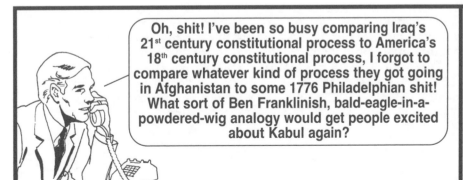 Oh, shit! I've been so busy comparing Iraq's 21st century constitutional process to America's 18th century constitutional process, I forgot to compare whatever kind of process they got going in Afghanistan to some 1776 Philadelphian shit! What sort of Ben Franklinish, bald-eagle-in-a-powdered-wig analogy would get people excited about Kabul again?

 It shouldn't be too hard to make a comparison. Just figure out which country everyone ignored in the 18th century, and add land mines.

August 29, 2005

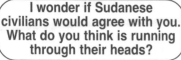You know, it used to bother me that Bush wasn't intervening to stop the genocide in Sudan— until I looked at Iraq.

I wonder if Sudanese civilians would agree with you. What do you think is running through their heads?

I know what's running through their heads: *"At least President Bush isn't over here somehow fucking this up and making it worse!"* And then they stop thinking, because they've been killed.

August 29, 2005

You know what would really help the average Iraqi? If everyone got a copy of the constitution, and it was actually a glass of clean drinking water.

Is there a way to print the constitution on a functioning electrical supply? That would be worth distributing to every Iraqi.

That's the nice thing about demo-cratic ideals—it's easy to say you're distributing them, and nobody can gauge whether you really are. Clean water, on the other hand? People are either drinking it, or they're not.

August 29, 2005

There should be a rule that if you slack off while an American city is destroyed, and then your response is to fly around hugging people and making excuses, you have to stop being President. And if it happens again four years later, you *really* have to stop.

Don't be so negative! I'm sure every-thing will work out and our nation will come together in strength, compassion and OH MY GOD IS THAT A BLOATED CORPSE FLOATING TOWARDS ME?

Anyway, yeah. The important thing is that we all work together to rebuild Trent Lott's house so Bush can sit on the porch so we can actually fucking find him next time.

September 15, 2005

September 15, 2005

September 15, 2005

September 15, 2005

September 15, 2005

September 15, 2005

September 15, 2005

September 20, 2005

September 26, 2005

September 26, 2005

"In view of the growing costs of Gulf Coast hurricanes, White House Budget Director Joshua Bolten said the president has asked him 'to examine the rest of the budget . . . to see where we can tighten our belt,' a quest that may lead to cuts in federal benefit programs. . . ." (The *Wall Street Journal*, 9/26/05)

Let's start by cutting food stamps and Medicaid. Then let's repeal the estate tax forever. Then, every two years, let's just drown all the poor people.

Forget *food* stamps— give the poor people *hug* stamps. Then, during the next disaster, they can cash them in for free hugs from the president!

You're naive. Those welfare people would just *abuse* hug stamps. They'd probably try to cash them in at strip clubs!

September 27, 2005

"In view of the growing costs of Gulf Coast hurricanes, White House Budget Director Joshua Bolten said the president has asked him 'to examine the rest of the budget . . . to see where we can tighten our belt,' a quest that may lead to cuts in federal benefit programs. . . ." (The *Wall Street Journal*, 9/26/05)

I hope they *do* cut federal benefit programs. If there's one thing Katrina showed us, it's that there are too many poor people just floating around.

Yeah—maybe a big cut in the food stamp program would motivate those lay-abouts to get jobs! (Once they're done decomposing in fetid water, of course.)

Poor people are obviously abusing their food stamps anyway— remember how they were always referred to as BLOATED corpses?

September 27, 2005

Where do you stand on the Iraqi constitution? Do you think it should be approved?

"Where do I stand?" As far as fucking physically possible away from it, hopefully. It looks to me like the constitution is the perfect recipe for civil war— *it's such a perfect recipe, you get the dish even if you don't actually USE the recipe.* It's like holding a cookbook up to a bucket of eggs, and ten minutes later you're eating a soufflé.

Whoa, hey—you're actually running out of ways to say Iraq is fucked up, aren't you?

October 4, 2005

October 10, 2005

October 10, 2005

October 18, 2005

Panel 1: What are you doing right now?

Panel 2: Reading about avian influenza, the Pakistan earthquake, and the Iraqi constitutional referendum.

Panel 3: Forget all that. *Let's go apple picking!* Just kidding. Did you read that article about how trapped carbon emissions are gonna lead to more deadly weather catastrophes?

October 18, 2005

Panel 4: There's a new CBS poll out saying 51% of Americans reject evolution and believe God created humans in their present form.

Panel 5: "In their present form?" Does that include the XXL sweatpants and yellow rubber bracelets and everything?

Panel 6: Yea verily. Remember Genesis 1:27— "... And then God created some LAZY-ASS motherfuckers whose fingers spent more time up their noses than they did flipping pages of their science homework."

October 25, 2005

Panel 7: Check out this sweet article in the *Daily News*: "Facing the darkest days of his presidency, President Bush is frustrated, sometimes angry and even bitter, his associates say."

Panel 8: "Frustrated, sometimes angry, and even bitter?" Jesus, *is Bush turning into a left-wing political cartoonist?*

Panel 9: No, I think he's still got a sense of humor.

October 25, 2005

OCTOBER, 2005 — *Waiting for the Fitzgerald indictments.*

(Boner)

October 28, 2005

"As the money runs out on the $30 billion American-financed reconstruction of Iraq, the officials in charge cannot say how many planned projects they will complete, and there is no clear source for hundreds of millions of dollars a year needed to operate the projects that have been finished . . ." (The *New York Times*, 10/30/05)

> Well, at least Scooter Libby was indicted! I'm sure that will help Iraqis. . . somehow.

> I think they should send Harriet Miers over to Iraq to fix everything. She is *really* organized. And polite. And she ain't got shit else to do.

> You know what sucks? Even if every incompetent asswipe in the White House is arrested, they all still get to live in America. Whereas the nicest, most decent Iraqi people have to live *in Iraq*.

October 30, 2005

"(T)he United States has spent $1.3 billion on reconstruction in Afghanistan, intending to win over Afghans with tangible signs of progress. . . . Meanwhile, the United States hopes to withdraw 4,000 soldiers from the country's south next spring; a drop in over-all foreign aid is expected; and Taliban attacks are rising. So both Afghan officials and foreign diplomats are assessing what has been achieved during the past four years, and **MANY ARE DISTURBED** by what they see." (*The New York Times*, 11/7/05)

> Want to make an extra $150,000 a year? Send one of your old tennis shoes over to Afghanistan to be a consultant for USAID. They could use the competence.

> The sad thing is, my grimy Reebok would probably have a crew of Afghans working under it. And it would probably be the most technologically advanced device in the neighborhood.

> Maybe if Bush added his Afghan approval ratings and his American approval ratings, he could actually outpoll broken car alarms and angry proctologists. . . for now.

November 7, 2005

Are we still winning over Afghans with our lovable and charming inability to get shit done for them?

Yeah, we're winning over Afghans. Who *doesn't* love flimsy-ass, ramshackle schoolhouses built years behind schedule that fuckin' fall apart if two students happen to fart simultaneously?*

*The overdue buildings aren't actually flimsy, but a conscientious cartoonist's first obligation is to fart jokes, not USAID.**

**United States Agency for International Development, which pays consultants $150,000 a year to chew tobacco and fuck around in countries with deserts.

November 7, 2005

"The Senate signaled its growing unease with the war in Iraq today, voting overwhelmingly to demand regular reports from the White House on the course of the conflict and on the progress that Iraqi forces are making. . . ." (*The New York Times,* 11/15/05)

They need regular reports *already?* Come on, it's only been two and a half years! Let's not rush things—it's just the Middle East!

I love that the Senate is demanding reports from the *White House,* as if all of a sudden the White House is capable of typing something that is true. *Umm, Senate? Maybe you should request some reports from IRAQIS, you idiots.*

Why bother with quarterly reports? If the Senate wants to get a sense of the situation in Iraq, they should just convene every ninety days to contemplate a gigantic, flaming pile of turds.

November 18, 2005

You know, everyone's debating whether we should cut and run in Iraq, but I'm starting to think we've *already* cut and run—in Afghanistan.

We wouldn't cut and run in Afghanistan— that preposition's wrong. We would cut and run *from* Afghanistan.

In, From, what difference does it make? Afghan kids can sort out the grammatical questions when we finish building their schools in three hundred years.

November 21, 2005

I'm tired of listening to Americans argue about withdrawing from Iraq in terms of what's best for America. Check the name of the war, guys—it's not "The America War." It's "The Iraq War." So maybe we should stop chewing our blankies and ask the Iraqis what would work best for *them*.

Oh, yeah? Which Iraqis are you gonna ask? The crazy-ass Sunnis who used to work for Saddam? The crazy-ass Shiites who are now torturing them? The Kurds? The old ladies who won't stop yelling about how we accidentally killed their kids? Come on, which Iraqis' wishes should we fulfill?

I don't know, damn—maybe the happy ones?

November 28, 2005

What's the best thing about being a genocidal murdering thug who gang-rapes little girls in Darfur?

Oh, man. The *best* thing? I don't know, what?

If you get a headache from the incessant screaming of your victims, you can always relax to the calming murmurs of White House disapproval. It's like the smooth jazz of genocide responses!

November 28, 2005

Ooh, I thought of another one! "The White House's reaction to Darfur has been as forceful and intimidating as a Thomas Kinkade painting floating in a bubblebath."

Come on, be fair. Bush has sent tons of humanitarian aid over there.

Well, that's a relief—nobody wants to be gang-raped on an empty stomach.

November 28, 2005

November 28, 2005

December 5, 2005

December 5, 2005

December 6, 2005

December 20, 2005

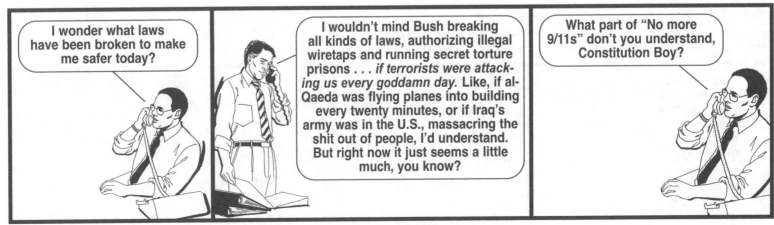

December 26, 2005

Panel 1: Umm. . . is there any form of communication the government *isn't* monitoring? I'm starting to think Bush couldn't follow the Fourth Amendment if he was on rollerblades and it was stapled to his dick.

Panel 2: You don't understand, dude: Bush didn't change the rules— *9/11 did.* We live in a post-9/11 world-environment reality. You're stuck in a pre-9/11 Constitution addiction situation. Get help.

Panel 3: Jesus Christ, enough with the 9/11 excuse!!! Why do citizens' balls *SPONTANEOUSLY FALL OFF* whenever that date comes up?

January 9, 2006

Panel 4: Why did twice as many American soldiers die in Afghanistan in 2005 than in 2004?

Panel 5: I don't know, why?

Panel 6: Because the Taliban is adopting techniques perfected by the Iraqi insurgency!

January 9, 2006

"With (Iraq) still a shambles, U.S. officials are promoting a tough-love vision of reconstruction that puts the burden on the Iraqi people. 'The world is a competitive place,' Tom Delare, economics counselor at the U.S. Embassy, said this month during a news briefing. 'You have to convince the investor that it is worth his while to put his money in your community.'" (*The LA Times*, 1/15/06)

Panel 7: Yeah! Come on and convince me, you lazy-ass Iraqis! Convince me to put money in your community!

Panel 8: Don't hold your breath, dude. Iraqis have lived under a centralized state-controlled economy for decades. *They don't understand that the world is a competitive place.* They should fly the same flag as the Special Olympics.

Panel 9: Wouldn't it be quicker if we just *literally beat Iraqis to death* with Ayn Rand books?

January 16, 2006

January 16, 2006

"After more than 2 1/2 years of sputtering reconstruction work, the United States' 'Marshall Plan' to rebuild [Iraq] is drawing to a close this year with much of its promise unmet and no plans to extend its funding. . . . [E]mbassy and reconstruction officials outlined a program of private investment and fiscal belt-tightening by the new Iraqi government as the long-term solution to the country's woes, even if that causes short-term suffering for Iraq's people. . . ." (*The Los Angeles Times,* 1/15/06)

January 17, 2006

January 23, 2006

 Did you hear the good news? ExxonMobil posted a $10.7 *billion* profit for the fourth quarter. It's a record! *We all win!*

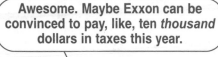 Awesome. Maybe Exxon can be convinced to pay, like, ten *thousand* dollars in taxes this year.

 But why should they have to pay taxes? It's not like this government ever did anything for them.

January 30, 2006

STATE OF THE UNION 2006!!! Yes indeed! The state of our union is STRONG!!! Strong like President Bush's MIND. Strong like an EXCLAMATION POINT.

 Oh my God! We're addicted to *oil*? And we're gonna cure that addiction by investing in some new-fangled type of *coal* plants? Can I cure my addiction to buffalo wings by moving into a sports bar?

 I got a cheaper idea — why not just shoot SUVs on sight?

I think you can only do that if Iraqi families are inside.

January 31, 2006

 What do you think of the White House's constitutional analysis? Did it convince you the NSA wiretaps are legal? Or were you maybe too busy wiping up Thomas Jefferson's ghost-vomit to notice?

 Here's George Bush's constitutional analysis: "I don't understand the fuckin' thing, so why should I obey it? It's written in some kind of loop-de-loop old-timey scribble-language anyway."

 Oh, I think he understands the Constitution, all right. It's the pre-9/11 nail he hangs his *Mr. Super President* cape on.

February 7, 2006

February 7, 2006

"Virtually every measure of the performance of Iraq's oil, electricity, water and sewerage sectors has fallen below preinvasion values even though $16 billion of American taxpayer money has already been disbursed in the Iraq reconstruction program..." (*The New York Times*, 2/9/06)

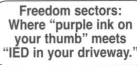

February 13, 2006

February 13, 2006

Panel 1 (February 20, 2006):

I read in the newspaper that we're making good progress training Iraqi security forces. And we're making progress diminishing sectarian tension!

Panel 2:

Sorry—after three years in Iraq, I don't get excited by the word "progress." That's some *bullshit.* Maybe I'd be excited by progress if we had only spent, like, two million dollars, or if we had a bunch of fifth-graders over there running the place for a fucking *science fair* or some shit. Then maybe I'd feel grateful for any ol' bit of good news that happened to drop out of the sky. But after all the money and time and bullshit we've burned through, I'm supposed to be thrilled for any moment we're not *ruining* Iraq? Ha! Fuck that and fuck "progress," where's "done"?

Panel 3:

I hope you know Thomas Friedman would be very disappointed to hear you say that!

February 20, 2006

Panel 4 (March 1, 2006):

Have you been following this Dubai controversy? I love that Bush didn't even know some creepy-ass government was gonna run our ports. Has anyone told him that Belgium stole all our space shuttles?*

*Not true!

Panel 5:

OK, wait—when did everybody decide to care about ports again? Didn't we all admit that the government would probably never check more than, like, 5% of all cargo ships? Hell, why do you think I moved hundreds of miles inland? And now everyone's like, *"Ooh! Ports! Wharves! Barges and boats! Suddenly we give a fuck!"*

Panel 6:

It's a good thing Dubai isn't in the organ-donor business—Bush would probably have us harvested for parts.

March 1, 2006

Panel 7 (March 6, 2006):

Did you watch Dennis Miller's new comedy special, where he places all the blame for the chaos in Iraq on . . . *Iraqi civilians*?

Panel 8:

Ah, Dennis Miller—the satirist whose grasp of foreign policy is as strong and sure as a baby's grip on a buttered anvil.

Panel 9:

I know! Since when does every has-been with a beard and a thesaurus get to play "world-affairs analyst?" Shit, I'd rather listen to Bill Kristol try to tell jokes than Dennis Miller try to explain Iraq.

March 6, 2006

"On Sunday, Marine Gen. Peter Pace, chairman of the Joint Chiefs of Staff, said in a televised interview that things in Iraq were 'going very, very well, from everything you look at.'" (*The Los Angeles Times,* 3/7/06)

 I like that he said "from EVERYTHING you look at." That means even if you look at, like, a random ceramic dolphin in an Iraqi shopkeeper's window, you'll see that things in Iraq are going very, very well.

Goddamn! The chairman of the Joint Chiefs must have access to some cutting-edge, high-tech, turbo-charged *super-soldier-ass* rose-colored glasses that make my crappy rose-colored glasses look like Kmart bifocals dipped in raspberry juice.

Or . . . he could just be a liar.

March 6, 2006

Eighty-five percent of our troops in Iraq say the U.S. mission is "to retaliate for Saddam's role in the 9/11 attacks."* Coincidentally, 85% of my time is now spent screaming, "*WHAT THE FUCK?*"

*Zogby poll, 2/28/06

Now it all makes sense! Of course we aren't winning in Iraq—*85% of our troops may be mentally retarded.*

Seriously, don't you think Bush is worried that so many soldiers are misinformed?

March 13, 2006

OK, here's our strategy for leaving Iraq: *As Iraqi troops stand up, U.S. troops will stand down.* It's like doing the Wave!

Fuck the Wave, when can we do the Macarena?

Actually, I think it's gonna be more like: *As Iraqi troops give up, U.S. troops will give up.*

March 13, 2006

NOTE: You may wonder why this comic doesn't make reference to the three-year anniversary of Operation Iraqi Freedom. Do you know why? *Because three-year anniversaries are BULLSHIT.* Come on, who celebrates a three-year wedding anniversary? *Only people who doubt they'll be married for four years.* Of course, our special relationship with Iraq will last much, much longer than that. So I'll make comics on the fifth, tenth, and twenty-fifth anniversaries of the Iraq war—and we'll be in Iraq to celebrate all of them. Hooray!

March 23, 2006

April 1, 2006

April 6, 2006

"A reconstruction contract for the building of 142 primary health centers across Iraq is running out of money, after two years and roughly $200 million, with no more than 20 clinics now expected to be completed. . ." (*The Washington Post*, 4/3/06)

I'm not worried about enough *health centers* getting built in Iraq—I'm worried about enough morgues getting built in Iraq. *For the love of God, what happens if they run out of morgues???*

Yeah. Worrying about whether there are enough functioning health clinics in Baghdad is like worrying about whether there are enough functioning karaoke machines at the Alamo—there's other shit to deal with first.

Seriously, who in Iraq has the time to make an appointment with a goddamn primary care physician? What the hell kind of sore throat could convince you to actually leave your house and try to get somewhere?

April 6, 2006

So Iran gets a nuclear weapon—who cares? Seriously, it's not like they'd ever use one. Ahmadinejad didn't run for president so he could get his country wiped off the face of the Earth.

You think Iran is just fucking with us so Bush will do something crazy and lose the rest of his credibility?

"The *rest* of his credibility"? What, did they find some leftovers in John McCain's mouth?

April 12, 2006

Everybody's saying Bush might bomb Iran soon, but I just don't see it. Then again, I didn't think Saddam Hussein was involved in 9/11, so what do I know?

It won't happen. If Bush is so crazy he'll bomb Iran, he's so crazy he'll insist we do it on Easter Sunday. And there's just not enough time between now and Sunday to come up with a kick-ass name for yet another war—let alone produce a gigantic "Mission Pre-ccomplished" banner.

Plus, he'd probably want to wait until the last day of his term to attack, just so he could walk out with an approval rating above 40%.

April 13, 2006

Panel 1: Am I really supposed to be impressed by a bunch of retired generals speaking out against Rumsfeld? Like it's cool for military guys to come to their senses five years too late?

Panel 2: Seriously, any military officer who didn't disagree, condemn, or raspberry Rumsfeld because they were worried about their *career* is probably too much of a pussy to do anything in this war other than collate stop-loss orders. Those anti-feather-rufflers can kiss a dick, for all I care. I'd rather have the troops led by Rosie O'Donnell and an angry pencil sharpener.

Panel 3: I bet that pencil sharpener would be really, really, really, *really* fucking expensive.

April 20, 2006

Panel 4: Did you hear about a bunch of Shiite militiamen moving into Kirkuk? They could battle Kurdish militias for control of the city.

Panel 5: To tell you the truth, I'm so sick of reading about ups and downs in Iraq I haven't opened a newspaper since February.

Panel 6: There have been ups?

*April 27, 2006**

Panel 7: Here's something I don't get: If God told Bush to invade Iraq, why didn't God stick around and tell him how to handle the postwar situation? What's up with *that*, God?

Panel 8: God is not responsible for Phase IV operations.

Panel 9: Damn! Not Him, either?

April 27, 2006

May 1, 2006

May 1, 2006

May 8, 2006

No wonder Bush wants Mexicans in the US—they're turning into crazy evangelicals who hate gay people!

That's why Republicans all over the country are tearing their hair out and yelling, "For the love of God, who do I fuckin' *fear first?*"

It's understandable—they're worried about Mexicans coming over here and stealing hate from *American* homophobes.

May 15, 2006

"Although Department of Defense standards for enlistment in the armed forces disqualify recruits who suffer from [Post-Traumatic Stress Disorder], the military is redeploying service members to Iraq who fit that criteria." (*The Hartford Courant*, 5/14/06)

Ahh, there's nothing like another tour of duty in Iraq to put your Iraq-induced post-traumatic stress disorder in perspective!

The fact that they're allowing people with PTSD to fight in Iraq makes me think the Department of Defense is actually recruiting *from the future*. So why not get some twenty-fifth century android super-soldiers up in here?

How long will it be before the military starts deploying soldiers who have already committed suicide?

May 15, 2006

"As chaos swept Iraq after the American invasion in 2003, the Pentagon began its effort to rebuild the Iraqi police with a mere dozen advisers. . . . Three years later, the police are a **BATTERED AND DYSFUNCTIONAL FORCE** that has helped bring Iraq to the brink of civil war. Police units stand accused of operating **DEATH SQUADS** for powerful political groups or simple profit." (*The New York Times*, 5/21/06)

Wow. A whole *dozen* advisers? We couldn't even spare a fucking *baker's* dozen?

Why is everyone complaining about for-profit death squads? I thought we were *supposed* to be encouraging free-market innovation in Iraq.

Yeah, the market is definitely removing inefficiencies. You might know them as "Sunnis."

May 22, 2006

"As chaos swept Iraq after the American invasion in 2003, the Pentagon began its effort to rebuild the Iraqi police with a mere dozen advisers. . . . Three years later, the police are a **BATTERED AND DYSFUNCTIONAL FORCE** that has helped bring Iraq to the brink of civil war." (*The New York Times,* 5/21/06)

So the Iraqi police force has brought Iraq to the brink of civil war? To the *brink?* Jeez, can't they finish *anything?*

How can Iraq be on the "brink" of civil war? Goddamn CIVIL WAR has a brink? I understand how, like, "al dente" has a brink you can approach in a pasta-based context, but civil war? A *brink?* I always thought civil war was like pregnancy—unbrinkable! No brink!

I used to think "spoon" was the weirdest word to say over and over—now I'm not so sure.

May 22, 2006

I agree with Thomas Friedman: When it comes to Iraq, the next six to nine months are really going to be *crucial.*

I'm sick of that line. Like any other six to nine months in Iraq *won't* be crucial? It's like saying, "The next six to nine slugs that enter your bullet-ridden skull are going to be *crucial.* Seriously, dude: Try to pay attention to those particular bullets."

You know how people have been saying that "six-to-nine months" line for years now? Do you think maybe they weren't referring to *consecutive* months?

May 29, 2006

They better finish appointing the Iraqi government before everyone in the country has been kidnapped or decapitated.

What if the secretary of the interior winds up being a bunch of random body parts collected in a bag and plopped on a chair?

I guess that wouldn't be so bad. Would an assortment of banged-up, bloody arms and legs *really* do a worse job than anyone else?

June 5, 2006

"The use of POTENT ANTIPSYCHOTIC DRUGS to treat children and adolescents for problems like aggression and mood swings increased more than fivefold from 1993 to 2002. . . . Only a HANDFUL OF SMALL STUDIES of the drugs have been completed in children and adolescents, whose BRAINS ARE STILL DEVELOPING. . . ." (*The New York Times*, 6/5/06)

So either American kids became five times more aggressive and moody in the years 1993 to 2002, or the drug industry became five times more greedy and evil. I gotta say, the kids look pretty normal to me. . . .

Hey, I've got an idea: Maybe kids are becoming more aggressive because adults are constantly trying to shove *untested pills* down their throats.

Children should get Pfizer stock options for each pill they swallow. That might help the moodiness.

June 7, 2006

"Afghan President Hamid Karzai said Sunday that his government would GIVE WEAPONS TO LOCAL TRIBESMEN so they could help fight the BIGGEST SURGE IN TALIBAN VIOLENCE in years." (*The Washington Post*, 6/11/06)

I've always said the one thing Afghanistan needs is more weapons in the hands of local tribesmen.

If local tribesmen are as responsible with their new weapons as they were with turning over al-Qaeda suspects to Guantanamo, Afghanistan is about to get superly-duperly stable.

If Afghanistan ever actually becomes stable, will Afghans *really* believe they're still in Afghanistan?

June 12, 2006

To cut, perchance to run. Ay, there's the rubble.

I love that the Republicans can reduce the concept of a phased withdrawal from Iraq to something that sounds like a goddamn *hairdresser-themed line dance.* "Hey DJ, put on some Dixie Chicks so me an' my girls can dance the Cut 'N' Run!"

Ha! So would that be some kind of goofy dance that actually kept people alive?

June 19, 2006

"The popularity of **IRAN'S CONTROVERSIAL LEADER,** Mahmoud Ahmadinejad, is surging almost a year after he unexpectedly won **CLOSELY CONTESTED PRESIDENTIAL ELECTIONS,** Iranian officials and Western diplomats said on Tuesday." (*The Guardian,* 6/20/06)

Ahmadinejad is such a cynical asshole! The scrawny idiot's been shaking his fist more than a craps addict on a losing streak. Is that the limit of his presidential ability?

Don't blame him, blame the Iranians. They get off on feeling threatened by us. They'd elect a goddamn piston-driven fist-shaking machine if they could.

What kind of freaks get off on *feeling threatened by other countries?*

June 20, 2006

"Many Afghans and some foreign supporters say they are **LOSING FAITH IN PRESIDENT HAMID KARZAI'S GOVERNMENT,** which is besieged by an escalating insurgency and endemic corruption and is **UNABLE TO PROTECT OR ADMINISTER** large areas of the country." (*The Washington Post,* 6/25/06)

Wow, people are starting to lose faith in Hamid Karzai's government? Are they already bored with riding fancy escalators at the Serena hotel?

Can we decide once and for all who we're gonna blame when Afghanistan implodes? Will it be Hamid Karzai or George Bush? NATO or the Taliban? When I play the blame game, I like to flip a coin, not roll a goddamn twelve-sided die.

Blame Saddam Hussein. If he hadn't been secretly developing WMDs and working with al-Qaeda, we never would have had to invade Iraq and lose focus in Afghanistan.

June 26, 2006

I love that Israel just straight-up *kidnapped* the Hamas government! Are we entering the "Natalee Holloway phase" of Israeli statecraft?

Oh, nice. I see you're enjoying some anti-Semitism along with your Fourth of July weiners. You probably don't even pronounce this month, since you think its first syllable owns all the banks.

You know, sometimes I think I actually *should* say something anti-Semitic, just so you'll see everybody rolling their eyes when you complain about it.

July 3, 2006

July 10, 2006

"Five years after the attacks on the United States, the Bush administration faces the prospect of **REWORKING KEY ELEMENTS OF ITS ANTI-TERRORISM EFFORT** in light of challenges from the courts, Congress and European allies crucial to counterterrorism operations." (*The Washington Post*, 7/11/06)

July 10, 2006

July 17, 2006

July 17, 2006

July 18, 2006

July 24, 2006

July 24, 2006

July 31, 2006

July 31, 2006

What do you think of Israel's strategy against Hezbollah?

It sounds good to me: Destroy the shit out of Lebanese towns until the locals resent Hezbollah for making Israel destroy the shit out of their towns.

That reminds me: Have the Guantánamo detainees decided to stop making us torture them yet?

August 2, 2006

What do you think of Israel's strategy against Hezbollah?

It sounds good to me: destroy the shit out of Lebanese towns until the locals resent Hezbollah for making Israel destroy the shit out of their towns.

It's enough to make me wish I owned stock in *shit-the-towns-are-destroyed-out-of.*

August 7, 2006

What do you think of Israel's strategy against Hezbollah?

It sounds good to me: destroy the shit out of Lebanese towns until the locals resent Hezbollah for making Israel destroy the shit out of their towns.

Ooh, what a clever strategy! A bunch of people will still get killed, right?

August 7, 2006

August 7, 2006

August 14, 2006

August 15, 2006

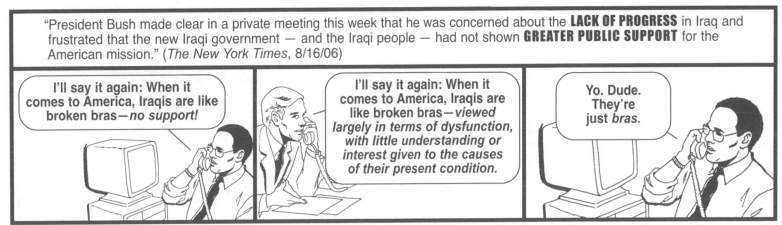

August 21, 2006

August 28, 2006

August 28, 2006

What if, on September 12th, we had immediately started rebuilding the towers—in secret, on their sides, so that a couple of months later we wheeled 'em into place in the middle of the night, and then raised them right up where the originals had stood. And so one morning bin Laden would've woken up to an assistant screaming, "*It was a dream! The towers are still standing!*" And everyone would have agreed to act like nothing had happened—that there had been a September 11th, but not a 9/11—just to screw with Osama. So the cave-dwellin' motherfucker's mind would have gone even bat-shittier than it already is, and he'd release a video saying, "What's the deal? Am I missing something here? Did I not totally knock down those goddamn infidel towers?" And we could have released our own videos: "Sorry, bro, don't know what you're talking about—our towers never went anywhere. Go rewind your Whitney Houston tapes."

Exactly! That way we could have focused from the start on the *real* mastermind behind 9/11: SADDAM HUSSEIN!

"Never forget . . . never learn shit."

August 30, 2006

NEVER FORGET...

. . . This is what a crying bald eagle looks like.

September 11, 2006

What did you do for the 9/11 anniversary?

I woke up, went to my crappy job, ate a flavorless crappy dinner, and fell asleep watching some crappy show on TV. And I was incredibly grateful for every crappy minute of it. What'd you do?

Umm. . . I forgot.

September 12, 2006

Panel 1: Did you like Bush's 9/11 anniversary speech?

Panel 2: Dammit! I *knew* there was something I was supposed to never forget to watch on TV! What did I miss?

Panel 3: You missed a guy who wishes he still had a megaphone. And a goddamn big pile of rubble to stand on.

September 12, 2006

"In the first days after the 9/11 attacks I promised to use **EVERY ELEMENT OF NATIONAL POWER** to fight the terrorists, wherever we find them. One of the strongest weapons in our arsenal is the **POWER OF FREEDOM.** The terrorists fear freedom as much as they do our firepower." (George W. Bush, 9/11/06)

Panel 1: Hmm. Is the Pentagon aware that terrorists fear freedom as much as our firepower? Because I'm looking at the FY 2006 military budget and we seem to be spending a shitload of money for something that's not even scarier than *freedom.*

Panel 2: You know what they say: "*Freedom without firepower is like a pleasant, abstract concept without the attendant mechanisms of violence which may actually undermine it.*"

Panel 3: Goddamn! When did they start saying *that?*

September 18, 2006

"The (9/11) attacks were meant to **BRING US TO OUR KNEES, AND THEY DID,** but not in the way the terrorists intended. Americans united in prayer, came to the aid of neighbors in need, and resolved that our enemies would not have the last word." —George W. Bush, 9/11/06

Panel 1: I remember coming to the aid of my neighbors on 9/11, but I'm pretty sure I wasn't *on my knees.* They're not that type of neighbors.

Panel 2: No, you jackass, that's not when you were on your knees— you were on your knees when we were united in prayer. Remember?

Panel 3: Oh, right. May I assume that after Bush's speech, we were all on our knees united in front of the toilet?

Hey, infidel, can I have the last word?

No!!!

September 18, 2006

September 18, 2006

September 25, 2006*

September 25, 2006

September 25, 2006

October 2, 2006

October 9, 2006

Panel 1 (October 9, 2006):

Goddamn. Iraq, Iran, and North Korea are totally beyond our control. Goddamn. *The Axis of Evil is actually kicking our asses.*

Why didn't we name the "Axis of Evil" the "Axis of Nations That Will Fuckin' Flummox the Fuck Out of Us and Totally Succeed at Whatever They Want to Do While We More or Less Stand by Helplessly?"

Why? Because we thought we would be able to *defeat evil.*

October 9, 2006

Panel 2 (October 16, 2006):

You know what kind of cartoon I would draw, if I could draw cartoons? I'd have the continental United States dressed up as Superman, about to jump off a ledge labeled "North Korea." But two old ladies named "China" and "Russia" would be standing below, shouting "*Wait! You're no longer a superpower!*" Oh—and North Korea would be dressed up as a bank robber, running away with a bag of money labeled "Nuclear tests."

Hold up—I thought North Korea was the ledge that USA-Superman was about to jump off. How can it also be a bank robber?

ARE YOU TELLING MY SYMBOLIC CARTOON VERSION OF NORTH KOREA WHAT TO DO?!?

October 16, 2006

Panel 3 (October 20, 2006):

Enough of this dicking around with parliaments and prime ministers and *process*—if Iraq wants to keep the lid on a civil war, it needs a good ol' goddamn ruthless strongman in charge. Purple fingerprints ain't cutting it.

I can think of two men who would have been perfect for holding Iraq together—unfortunately, we killed Uday and Qusay Hussein. I knew de-Baathification was a mistake!

So where do you find the right kind of megalomaniacal psycho with enough best-practice brutality to save Iraq? Monster.com?

October 20, 2006

October 23, 2006

October 23, 2006

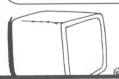

October 30, 2006

Did you have any problems voting on Tuesday?

"Problems voting?" You mean like long lines, or broken Tetris-ass video-game voting machines, or whatever?

No—I mean, Did you have any problems finding a candidate you actually wanted to vote for?

November 6, 2006

First Republicans lose Congress, and now Rumsfeld's out? Who cancelled Happy Hour at the Quagmire Cafe? Rumsfeld never even got to complete his TRANSFORMATION OF MILITARY AFFAIRS!

You mean his transformation of the United States military into an unstoppable war-losing machine? You really want Rumsfeld to finish the job on that?

Maybe you're right. Anyway, I'm sure he'll have fun revolutionizing the pudding matrix at his nursing home's cafeteria.

November 8, 2006

I miss hating him already.

November 8, 2006

Strip 1:

"Insurgent activity in Afghanistan has risen fourfold this year, and militants now launch more than 600 attacks a month, **A RISING WAVE OF VIOLENCE** that has resulted in 3,700 deaths in 2006. . ." —*Associated Press*, 11/13/06

Jeez, you think maybe the Baker-Hamilton commission could spend a few minutes dealing with Afghanistan? The fuckin' *handbasket* that place is going to hell in must be approaching the speed of sound.

Interesting theory. And what happens when a hellbound hand-basket actually breaks the sound barrier? Does it wind up *behind* the explosions pushing it along?

Hell, I don't know. Why don't you ask the goddamn Baker-Hamilton commission? I'm sure those *impossible-problem-solving, magical middle-aged men* could fix my stupid metaphor.

November 13, 2006

Strip 2:

"Whatever your opinion of the outcome (last Tuesday), all Americans can take pride in the **EXAMPLE OUR DEMOCRACY SETS FOR THE WORLD** by holding elections even in a time of war." —President Bush, 11/11/06

Yeah, I think we really blew the world's mind when we held elections last week.

The world was all like, "How is America gonna pull off *actually holding elections?* Don't those crazy kids know it's a *time of war?*" And America was all like, "Check out this intense example we're setting! *Plunk!* I just totally pulled a lever! DEAL WITH IT!"

Holy shit, I know why Bush thinks it's a big deal we held elections— somebody told him Iraq invaded *us.*

November 13, 2006

Strip 3:

"According to a new report by a commission of Afghan and foreign officials, **INSURGENT AND TERRORIST ATTACKS** nationwide have **INCREASED FOURFOLD** in the past year, reaching 600 incidents per month by September and causing 3,700 deaths since January." (*The Washington Post*, 11/20/06)

What the fuck is up with us *un-winning* Afghanistan? Are we throwing the game? Is NATO, like, the Chicago Black Sox of foreign intervention?

We're still winning—we're just changing the spread.

Do you think we'd still use sports metaphors to talk about war if baseball games ended with civilians' blown-up body parts strewn all over the field?

November 20, 2006

"The White House again resisted assertions that **IRAQ IS NOW IN A CIVIL WAR,** but that stance is increasingly hard to defend, according to analysts, diplomats and even some U.S. officials in private." (*The Washington Post*, 11/27/06)

OK, maybe we should ask the White House to take baby steps: Don't say Iraq is in a "civil war." Start by saying it's in a "schmivil schmwar."

What the hell difference does it make what people call it? It's not like Iraqis will become magically un-decapitatable once they're officially in a "civil war." Iraq's infrastructure is not suddenly gonna say, "Holy smokes, you mean this is a CIVIL WAR? Well, then, I'll just go ahead and fix *myself.*"

Yeah, but once Iraq's in a civil war, we can tell ourselves it's not our fault.

November 27, 2006

Why are people so determined to hear Bush admit that Iraq is in a "civil war?" Why are we peering at that pile-of-shit situation through the goddamn *goggles of wordplay?* Is this country being run by English majors all of a sudden?

But words matter: Remember what happened when the White House finally declared Darfur a genocide? We brought that shit to a *screeching halt.*

Oh, so all the screeching in Darfur is from a *halt?* I thought it was from women being gang-raped by janjaweed.

November 27, 2006

Did Vladimir "Voldemort" Putin *really* poison somebody with radiation? He's into some fiendish shit these days!

Yeah. And the crazy thing is, when Bush looked into Putin's soul a few years ago, he actually *foresaw it happening.*

Wow. Why didn't he warn anyone?

BECAUSE BUSH AIN'T NO SNITCH!

December 4, 2006

We could have won the war in Iraq if the media hadn't sided with the terrorists. As far as the safety of our troops is concerned, the *New York Times* is just another improvised explosive device.

So if we lived in a nation with no newspapers and no magazines, we would have won in Iraq *when?*

Well, see, now it gets complicated—because to *really* win in Iraq, we'd also need to live in a world with no internet, no calendars, no sectarian dynamics, no disillusioned Iraqis, no disenfranchised Iraqis, and no other Iraqis.

December 4, 2006

"Some Afghans view groups that advocate women's emancipation as **THE REAL DANGER TO SOCIETY** and blame foreign influence for provoking the widely reported phenomenon of **SELF-IMMOLATION** by unhappy brides or daughters-in-law." (*The Washington Post*, 12/5/06)

Wasn't the plan to turn Afghanistan into some kind of pro-American, free-market, progressive utopia? Like, the Central Asian equivalent of a Missouri Wal-Mart run by Women's Studies professors?

Yes. And if we hadn't rushed off and invaded Iraq, Afghanistan would be in better shape. Maybe we'd see fewer Afghan girls setting themselves on fire.

When an Afghan girl sets herself on fire, she probably thinks, "*Being Afghan sucks. If I was in Iraq, someone else would do this for me.*" Oh, and by the way: the theory you expressed in the second panel is loopy optimistic bullshit.

December 5, 2006

"A watchdog group that promotes religious freedom in the U.S. military accused senior officers on Monday of using their rank and influence to **COERCE SOLDIERS AND AIRMEN** into adopting **EVANGELICAL CHRISTIANITY**." (*Reuters*, 12/11/06)

Is this *really* the best time for American military officers to be promoting evangelical Christianity?

Are you kidding? Hell, I wish the Pentagon had entered the proselytization game years ago! I hope they bring the same tactical brilliance to *coercively promoting evangelical Christianity* that they brought to *stabilizing Iraq*. Do you know why? BECAUSE THEN THE ENTIRE FUCKIN' FAITH TRADITION WILL BE ACCIDENTALLY DESTROYED BEYOND RECOGNITION IN THREE YEARS.

Maybe. . . but wouldn't you always want to wait another three to six months, just to be sure?

December 12, 2006

"Over the past six months, Baghdad has been **ALL BUT ISOLATED ELECTRICALLY,** Iraqi officials say, as insurgents have **EFFECTIVELY WON THEIR BATTLE** to bring down critical high-voltage lines and cut off the capital from the major power plants to the north, south and west." (*The New York Times*, 12/19/06)

I'm glad Baghdad doesn't have much electricity. If Iraqis don't have electricity, they can't watch television and be fooled by all the absurdly negative reporting about Iraq.

But what about newspapers? Newspapers don't run on electricity!

True. And that's exactly why as soon as we invaded, we should have scooped out Iraqis' eyes and ears and kept 'em all in a big bucket until the media learned how to report good news.

December 19, 2006

"The Bush administration is split over the idea of **A SURGE IN TROOPS TO IRAQ,** with White House officials aggressively promoting the concept over the **UNANIMOUS DISAGREEMENT** of the Joint Chiefs of Staff, according to U.S. officials familiar with the intense debate." (*The Washington Post*, 12/19/06)

I think it'd be cool to send 15,000 more troops to Iraq in a big surge—IF the troops yelled "*Surge! Surge!*" the entire time.

I actually think those troops should utilize the shock and awe of a gerund: "*Surging! Surging!*" Let's see Iraqis deal with *that*.

Well, the important thing is, once those additional troops surge into Iraq, they will make a HUGE FUCKING DIFFERENCE.

December 19, 2006

I hate "Surge!" "Surge" sounds like a goddamn waterpark in Ohio or some shit. I liked it better a few weeks ago, when the cool thing to say about Iraq was "*Go big, go long, or go home.*" Now *that's* a phrase that makes me sound like I know what the fuck I'm talking about when I utter it.

I think they should combine every recent Iraq-related phrase into one ultimate phrase, like: "*Surge big, surge long, or clear-and-hold home.*" That sounds good!

Don't forget Thomas Friedman's stupid new goddamn phrase: "*Ten months or ten years.*" Throw that in: "*Surge ten go big, surge long go years ten, or months clear ten-and-hold home!*" You know—all of a sudden (*sniff*)... I actually think we can win this motherfucker.

December 21, 2006

Are you looking forward to the new year?

Hell yes! 2006 was a bullshit year. It felt like the first year in the War on Terror in which nothing really big happened—things just sort of pooped along. You know, I think I'm actually getting *bored* with this generation-defining, high-stakes battle for the future of civilization.

You know, for something so boring, you'd be surprised at how much it's gonna cost.

December 21, 2006

Do you think 2006 will be remembered as the year we lost Iraq?

No, I think 2006 will be remembered as the year before the year we *won* Iraq—with our new way forward and our bold new surge-vision for victory and new goal-achievement.

Hmm. I think 2006 will be remembered as the year thirty years before the year we left Iraq.

December 21, 2006

I heard an Iraqi in Dearborn say hanging Saddam justified *the entire Iraq war.*

Umm. . . for all the money we've spent, couldn't they have hung him with more panache? That was the dingiest state execution I've ever seen! The thing looked like it took place in a CBGB's bathroom!

Meanwhile, somewhere in western Pakistan...

Hurry up! The sooner we get this on YouTube, the funnier it'll be!

January 1, 2007

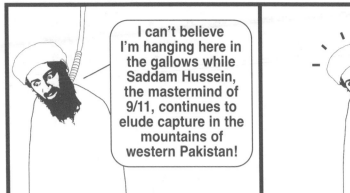

I can't believe I'm hanging here in the gallows while Saddam Hussein, the mastermind of 9/11, continues to elude capture in the mountains of western Pakistan!

Wait a minute— did I get that right?

January 1, 2007

I heard Tony Blair won't commit additional British troops to SURGE 2007!

Why would you want to miss out on SURGE 2007? You'll totally be kicking yourself in twenty years. The t-shirts alone will be collector's items!

Someday, National Guardsmen on their twentieth straight rotation will be like, "This new SURGE 2027 can't hold a candle to the original. SURGE 2007 just had a special vibe that can't be recaptured. You shoulda been there, bro." And they'll get all misty-eyed.

January 8, 2007

How many additional troops would have to go to Iraq before it affected you personally?

Hmm. I don't really know anyone in the military, so. . . maybe, like, a million troops? Maybe if they recruited a million more troops I would know one of 'em? And then maybe I'd *finally* bother learning the difference between a battalion and a brigade. Right now, I define both words as: "*a large group of armed strangers*."

See? That's why I think they should call up *fifty* million troops. Not to mention, we would totally win the *FUCK* out of the war then.

January 8, 2007

Strip 1 (January 15, 2007):

Panel 1:
Hey, bro, remember me? I'm that ol' hippie who was always out on the corner with his "NO WAR" sign. Remember? You and your high-school friends used to yell at me when you drove by?

Panel 2:
I tried telling you 'n' your buds about the military-industrial complex, but you laughed and told me to "go suck some patchouli"? Remember? Anyway, kid, I just wanted to say one thing:

Panel 3:
Have a nice surge.

This has been a presentation of "Mean Ol' Hippie Comics."

January 15, 2007

Strip 2 (January 16, 2007):

"In the days before Secretary of State Condoleezza Rice met with officials in Egypt, the news media here were filled with stories detailing charges of **CORRUPTION, CRONYISM, TORTURE AND POLITICAL REPRESSION**. . . . It was clear that the United States—facing chaos in Iraq, rising Iranian influence and the destabilizing Israeli-Palestinian conflict—had decided that **STABILITY, NOT DEMOCRACY,** was its priority. . . ." (*The New York Times*, 1/15/07)

Panel 1:
Why are we changing our priority from democracy to stability? Can't we have both?

Panel 2:
You know what I think our priority should be? _Perfection._ LET'S GO FOR IT!!!

Panel 3:
Seriously, though: Wasn't democracy supposed to bring stability? I'm really, seriously asking you why things got so fucked up.

January 16, 2007

Strip 3 (January 16, 2007):

Iraqi Crybaby Theatre

Panel 1:
Waah! The bad Americans blowed up my country!

Panel 2:
More than 30,000 Iraqis got dead last year! Boo-hoo! I want everything to get better *right now!*

Panel 3:
Give it a rest! Nobody likes a crybaby.

January 16, 2007

January 18, 2007

January 18, 2007

January 18, 2007

Iraqi Crybaby Theatre

It's strange that doctors are leaving Iraq, because there is actually quite a high demand for them right now.

Waah! I'm a big baby who can't appreciate irony!

I BLAME AMERICA!!!

January 18, 2007

Iraqi Crybaby Theatre

Waah! Why can't America make everything perfect for me?

Boo-hoo! Waah! Waah!

I wonder what they're having for lunch at the American Enterprise Institute?

January 18, 2007

Why are middle-class Iraqis in such a hurry to leave their country?

I know! It's like: Be patient, guys—we haven't even finished invading you yet!

When Iraq's entire professional class has abandoned the country, *that's* when I think we should REALLY start blowing it up.

January 22, 2007

Strip 1 — February 12, 2007

Are you following the Scooter Libby trial?

I tried, but the menagerie of *nation-ruining assholes* involved made it too painful. Besides, I already know enough to hate all the key players unconditionally.

Yeah, but following the trial might help you calibrate your disgust.

OH NO! You mean I might be *over-loathing* Tim Russert by 5%? Dude, I'm not some ham-radio motherfucker in his basement trying to dial in the perfect frequency. My contempt is in its "blunt object" phase, y'know?

February 12, 2007

Strip 2 — February 13, 2007

So I've decided to *totally* support us attacking Iran. I should back at least *one* of these wars, right?

You really know how to pick a winner. I hear Iranians are already getting their rose petals in order.

I was starting to feel like a chess-club nerd trapped in a homecoming week that wound up lasting five years. But I'm finally ready to be a war cheerleader!

Funny, these pom-poms smell like Joe Lieberman.

February 13, 2007

Strip 3 — February 20, 2007

"Senior leaders of Al Qaeda operating from Pakistan have **RE-ESTABLISHED SIGNIFICANT CONTROL** over their once-battered **WORLDWIDE TERROR NETWORK** and over the past year have set up a band of training camps in the tribal regions near the Afghan border. . ." (*The New York Times*, 2/18/07)

I thought the whole reason we invaded Iraq was to draw out the terrorists. What the fuck are they still doing over in Pakistan? Are they so goddamn dumb they can't find Iraq on a map?

Maybe we could send a bunch of school buses to Waziristan, load them up with terrorists, and drive their asses to Iraq, field-trip style. Then just shoot 'em as they step off the bus.

Seriously, *why are these scrawny fuckin' numbskull terrorists still outwitting us???* I'm starting to feel like we're living in some kind of fucking Aesop's fable!

February 20, 2007

"The White House signaled its growing impatience with Pakistan's **FAILURE TO CRACK DOWN ON ISLAMIC EXTREMISTS,** dispatching Vice President Cheney . . . to pressure President Pervez Musharraf to do more against a resurgent Taliban and al-Qaeda fighters."
(*The Washington Post*, 2/27/07)

So Cheney's finally putting the screws to ol' Pervez about al-Qaeda—and not a moment too soon! I was getting worried.

Just to be clear: Are you aware this is February of 2007, *not* February of 2001?

WOW. I guess Cheney's running a little behind schedule. Thank God he's the smartest man in the world, right?

February 27, 2007

I think we should be grooming al-Qaeda, not fighting them. They're Sunni; they could invade Iran for us.

Why would al-Qaeda invade Iran? Because Iran is Shiite?

Exactly! Isn't it obvious?

Ever since I learned there's a difference between Shiites and Sunnis, I've become a total strategic genius!

February 27, 2007

I love that this whole U.S. attorney-purge thing has brought Harriet Miers back into the spotlight! She's my girl!

For the love of God, why isn't that woman sitting on the Supreme Court?

Honestly? She isn't sitting on the Supreme Court because she's not all that bright.

March 13, 2007

March 14, 2007

March 20, 2007

March 26, 2007*

March 26, 2007

March 26, 2007

April 2, 2007

Strip 1:

Does President Ahmadinejad actually *want us* to invade Iran? He's sure acting like it!

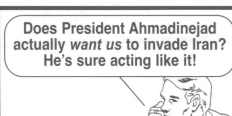

I can't tell. Maybe he's just fucking around because he's bored—the diplomatic equivalent of sticking frogs in a microwave.

If he's so bored, why doesn't that Casual Friday-lookin' motherfucker learn to crack the Windsor knot?

April 2, 2007

Strip 2:

"Tens of thousands of protesters loyal to Moktada al-Sadr, the Shiite cleric, took to the streets of the holy city of Najaf . . . in an extraordinarily disciplined rally to demand an end to the American military presence in Iraq. . . ." (*The New York Times,* 4/9/07)

Goddamn, that was some anti-war march! Aren't Iraqis afraid of people saying they don't support our troops?

You know what I liked about that Iraqi anti-war march? No "FREE MUMIA" signs.

That's ironic, since they probably have more Mumias than we do.

April 10, 2007

Strip 3:

Can you believe Nancy Pelosi went to Syria?

Are you kidding? At this point I'm surprised I haven't tried to go to Syria. If nobody in the White House is gonna do shit to solve anything, why not? At least Pelosi is willing to discuss foreign policy in actual foreign places.

So if she's just trying to help, why is the White House so mad?

They're mad because they *have no idea what they're doing.*

April 10, 2007

April 10, 2007

April 16, 2007

April 17, 2007*

Panel 1: I was sorry to hear they're not going to build that "security wall" in Baghdad.

Panel 2: I'm surprised Iraqis didn't want another wall. Aren't they running out of surfaces to write anti-American graffiti on?

Panel 3: Not to mention, what kind of idiots turn down a FREE WALL?

April 23, 2007

"Of the nearly 24,000 wounded soldiers returning from Iraq and Afghanistan, about a third suffer from some degree of **TRAUMATIC BRAIN INJURY**. . . . A newly-appointed **COMMISSION ON CARE FOR AMERICA'S RETURNING WOUNDED WARRIORS** was formed by U.S. President George Bush in response." (*Reuters*, 4/23/07)

Panel 1: *"America's Returning Wounded Warriors?"* If you joined the Army because you wanted to go to college, are you *really* a warrior?

Panel 2: Just contemplating the dumb-ass names they come up with for commissions will give you a traumatic brain injury.

Panel 3: Some poor kid lying in a hospital bed is supposed to be impressed he's a *"wounded warrior"?* Actually, he'd probably appreciate it—if his brain wasn't all fucked up.

April 23, 2007

Iraqi Crybaby Theatre

Panel 1: *Boo-hoo!* All the American reconstruction projects are falling apart!

Panel 2: I thought America was going to help Iraq, but the whole country is collapsing! *Waah!*

Panel 3: (Being a crybaby and complaining helps me forget that my entire family has been slaughtered.)

April 30, 2007

"[I]nspectors for a federal oversight agency have found that in a sampling of eight projects that the United States had declared successes [in Iraq], seven were **NO LONGER OPERATING** as designed. . ." (*The New York Times*, 4/29/07)

Why are we still trying to rebuild stuff in Iraq?

Because this is a *humanitarian war!* The whole point is to help Iraqis. That means painting hospitals and paving roads.

Paving roads? Too complicated. Instead, let's focus on democratizing a region whose history and culture totally bewilder us. That should be a snap, if we can't even *keep the shit we fixed actually fixed.*

April 30, 2007

"Doonesbury Style"

Mr. President, recent polls show Americans are unhappy with your leadership.

Which parts of my leadership are they unhappy with?

The parts where you fucking suck shit.

Oh dear!

April 30, 2007

George Tenet's doing all right for himself, huh? $4 million book deal, $2 million from the security industry. . . . Meanwhile, American and Iraqi teenagers are still busy killing each other in 100-degree heat.

***Boohoo, rich assholes profit from war while other people's kids do the fighting.* You know what, Mr. Grumpy McLenin? Tenet's not the only one making out like a bandit.**

Right, I almost forgot: Our troops are getting months' more free MREs than they expected.

May 8, 2007*

Why is everybody breathing down Bush's neck, forcing him to prove Iraq has turned a corner? We didn't defeat the Nazis overnight, you know!

Dude, we've been fighting in Iraq longer than we fought in World War II.

But that just proves George W. Bush is a mightier warrior than Franklin D. Roosevelt!!!

May 8, 2007

Well, it's not like we've had *half a decade* to figure out how to kill the Taliban without pissing off regular Afghans—we've only had five years.

We'll get it right eventually. Rome wasn't bombed-the-shit-out-of in a day.

Back in 2001, I was really excited to attack Afghanistan and kill all the Taliban—I never thought it would actually be *complicated*.

May 14, 2007

Two million Iraqis have fled the country. *That's a lot of quitters.*

Yeah, I don't like fair-weather fans. Abandoning their team just because it's hit a bit of a cold streak? Lame.

You know, for some reason I think "hot streak" would be a more descriptive phrase.

May 14, 2007

Are you gonna vote for Rudy Giuliani, "America's Mayor?"

You know, anyone dumb enough to call Giuliani "America's Mayor" probably thinks America *actually has a mayor*.

I'm reading TIME magazine's 2001 "Man of the Year" article about him: *A very human man taught us super-human courage.* Did you know TIME plagiarized from inspirational kitten posters in orthodontist's offices?

May 21, 2007

"The Iraq war, which for years has drawn militants from around the world, is beginning to **EXPORT FIGHTERS AND THE TACTICS THEY HAVE HONED** in the insurgency to neighboring countries and beyond . . ." (*The New York Times*, 5/28/07)

Great: Iraq has turned into a fuckin' finishing school for terrorists. I wonder if they get little diplomas before heading out to blow shit up in other countries?

What would it take to convince those guys to stay in Iraq and continue their studies on-campus?

Maybe a really good intramural basketball program?

May 28, 2007

I saw a new ad for the National Guard. How come they never show anyone training in a desert?

They show people training in the snow; in a jungle; in the woods—in every goddamn ecosystem on Earth except the one they'll actually be fighting in.

Is *that* why we can't conquer Iraq? Because our people are going over there thinking they're gonna be dealing with *icicles* and fuckin' *mittens* and shit?!?

June 4, 2007

June 4, 2007

June 5, 2007

June 12, 2007

The new military push around Baghdad has been dubbed "OPERATION ARROWHEAD RIPPER."

Holy shit, that's one of the toughest names yet! It makes me think of someone so bad-ass, he actually *FARTS ARROWHEADS.*

Can't we just cut the bullshit and call it "Operation Manifest Destiny?"

June 19, 2007

"(M)ore than four years into the war in Iraq, as many as **FOUR IN 10 AMERICANS** (41 percent) still believe Saddam Hussein's regime was **DIRECTLY INVOLVED** in financing, planning or carrying out the terrorist attacks on 9/11. . ."
(Newsweek, 6/23/07)

Well, now I know what it feels like to wish that FOUR IN TEN Americans would immediately kill themselves. It feels bad.

Oh, come on: Think of how easy parking will be!

The thing that makes my head hurt is *more people think Saddam caused 9/11 than approve of Bush's job performance.* I mean, what the heck do you *do* with a factoid like that?

June 25, 2007

What kind of Keystone-Cop, country-bumpkin-ass terrorists are running around Great Britain these days? Trying to *crash a car into an airport,* like that's gonna be dramatic?

Seriously! I'm like, "Dudes, it's a freaking AIRPORT. It's filled with AIRPLANES. Crash one of *them,* you no-ambition motherfuckers."

Ooh, I bet next they'll try crashing a flashlight into an IKEA store! *That'll* scare people.

July 3, 2007

July 3, 2007

July 10, 2007

"With little fanfare, at least so far, the stage is being set for a post-'surge' Iraq strategy that **REDUCES U.S. AMBITIONS** for the Iraq project, even while keeping some US forces there for years to come."

(*The Christian Science Monitor*, 7/9/07)

July 10, 2007

"Inspectors from the United Nations nuclear watchdog agency have confirmed that North Korea has shut down its weapons-making nuclear reactor, the agency said today." (*The New York Times,* 7/16/07)

A positive development in foreign policy? From the Bush administration? Seriously, what's the catch?

The catch is, all our heads are gonna explode trying to comprehend this.

Of course! And then Kim Jong Il flies in on his mechanical monkey to *FEED ON OUR EXPOSED BRAINS!* We got played *again.*

July 16, 2007

Don't you think we should invade Pakistan and root out all the al-Qaeda people living in the woods?

I really don't care. I don't live near a skyscraper, or a nuclear power plant—how's al-Qaeda gonna hurt me?

Dude, they could DROP A NUCLEAR BOMB OUT OF A SUITCASE ON YOU!!!

July 17, 2007

Is there a difference between al-Qaeda and al-Qaeda in Iraq?

"Al-Qaeda" are the assholes who attacked us on 9/11. "Al-Qaeda in Iraq" is a newer, more Iraq-ish collection of assholes.

But President Bush says "al-Qaeda in Iraq" are the same people who attacked us on 9/11.

Yeah, well—he *would* say that, wouldn't he?

July 17, 2007

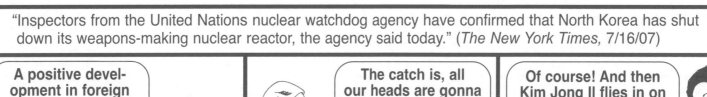

"If we had those 40 million (aborted) children that were killed over the last 30 years, **WE WOULDN'T NEED THE ILLEGAL IMMIGRANTS** to fill the jobs that they are doing today."
—Former House Majority Leader Tom DeLay, 7/13/07

Oh come on, DeLay—how is an aborted fetus gonna push a lawnmower?

I think DeLay meant that if the aborted fetuses had *grown up*, they could've mowed the lawn.

Ah! When he said, *If we had those children*, I thought he meant like, *If we had them stacked up in a huge messy pile.*

July 24, 2007

"Americans' support for the initial invasion of Iraq has risen somewhat as the White House has continued to ask the public to **RESERVE JUDGMENT ABOUT THE WAR** until at least the fall." (*The New York Times*, 7/24/07)

Support for the invasion has *risen?* So why does the White House to ask the public to "reserve judgment?" People can't reserve something they *don't have.*

Americans need to *seriously* wise the heck up, before I turn into one of those super-bitter weirdos who wears a denim vest covered in scary political buttons and calls people "sheeple."

I know—much more of this, and I'll be the first C.P.A. soccer mom to ever hand out flyers at the anarchist book fair.

July 24, 2007

What do you think about this huge arms deal we're gonna do with Saudi Arabia?

I like it. Saudi Arabia has been a steadfast ally in the War on. . . Umm. . . Shoot, this is embarrassing: I can't remember what it's called. Is it "War on *Terror?*"

Dude, If you honestly forgot what the War on Terror was called, I would totally marry you.

July 30, 2007

I'm *glad* we're selling $20 billion in weapons to Saudi Arabia. I like those guys.

What do you like about them?

Well, for one thing, they have great taste in weapons!

July 31, 2007

What do you think of Congressman Tom Tancredo's suggestion that we bomb Mecca and Medina if there's another terror attack?

It's a step in the right direction. I actually think we should destroy *all* religious holy sites.

If there's a terror attack?

Sure! Or if there's not.

August 7, 2007

"On the eve of his Camp David meeting with Mr. Bush, Mr. Karzai painted a **BLEAK PICTURE** of life in (Afghanistan), saying that **SECURITY HAD WORSENED** and that the United States and its allies were no closer to catching Mr. bin Laden than they were a few years ago." (*The New York Times*, 8/6/07)

I always wonder what Hamid Karzai's thinking when he boards that plane back to Afghanistan.

He's probably feeling grateful for all we've done to help his country.

I assume it's more like, "*Does this goddamn plane fly anywhere other than Afghanistan?*"

August 7, 2007

CORMAC IGNATIEFF'S "THE ROAD"

Hello everyone! Personal message to all the New Yorkers out there: Did you read Michael Ignatieff's essay in the 8/5/07 *NY Times Magazine*? If so, contact me ASAP to let me know you're OK. I put your flyer up at Grand Central Station, but have heard no response.

Myself, I'm just making my way out of the debilitating Level-Five Mind Fog that came from reading the thing. Even my "Second Life avatar" has a headache! (Hey young people, did I get that right? Hope so. See you in "Warcraft Worlds!")

The essay is called "Getting Iraq Wrong." And baby, if Michael Ignatieff got Iraq wrong, I don't want him to be right! Because this essay can MAKE LEMONADE IN YOUR MIND.

I wrote a cyber-essay about Ignatieff a couple years ago. The cyber-essay was called "My Old Bus Stop" (when I lived in Boston, I caught the #66 bus in front of Harvard's Kennedy School, where Ignatieff taught). It concerned itself with a masterpiece of foreign policy fan fiction: Ignatieff's 2005 *NY Times Magazine* essay justifying the Iraq war. Ignatieff's essay was called "Let's All Fly Up in Space and Smoke Dope Together." (That was the vibe, anyway.)

In that 2005 essay, you'll recall, Ignatieff said the reason the American public wanted to invade Iraq was to spread "The Ultimate Task of Thomas Jefferson's Dream." (I am not making a joke. This is for real.) And, he implied, anyone who opposed the invasion of Iraq did so because they hated Thomas Jefferson—and they didn't believe in the Ultimate Tasks of Dreams!

So far, so GREAT, right?

Ignatieff's latest essay is what Latin people call a "mea culpa," which is Greek for "Attention publishers: I am ready to write a book about the huge colossal mistake I made." I imagine the book will be about a man struggling to do the right thing—a man who thinks with his heart and dares, with a dream in each fist, to reach for the stars. It's about a journey: a journey from idealistic, starry-eyed academic to wizened, war-weary politician. (Ignatieff left Harvard; now he's Prime Chancellor of Canada's Liberal Delegate or whatever kind of wack-ass, kumbaya government they've got up there.)

In a way, it's a story much like Cormac McCarthy's recent best-selling *The Road*. Both follow a hero's long march through thankless environments—in Ignatieff's case, from the theory-throttled, dusty tower of academia to the burned-out hellhole of representative politics. Danger lurks. Grime abounds. The narrative tension is: Can the hero be wrong about everything, survive, and still convince everyone he's smarter than the Moveon.org people?

I was excited when I first saw this new essay: At last, Ignatieff was going to come clean about his super-duper-double-dipper errors. I expected a no-holds barred, personal excoriation. In fact, I assumed the first, last, and only sentence of the essay would be: "*Please, for the love of God, don't ever listen to me again.*"

HOWEVER . . .

The first nine-tenths of Ignatieff's essay, far from being an honest self-examination, is a collection of vague aphorisms and bong-poster koans. It hums with the comforting murmur of lobotomy. I refuse to believe this section was actually written by a member of the Canadian government, because that would mean Canada is even more "fuxxor3d" than America. (A little hacker-speak, that. There will be more; I finally bought the B3rlitz tapes.)

Below, a smorgasbord of Ignatieff's musings, with commentary:

An intellectual's responsibility for his ideas is to follow their consequences wherever they may lead. A politician's responsibility is to master those consequences and prevent them from doing harm . . .

Right off the bat, he's saying: "It was right for me to support the Iraq war when I was an academic, because academics live in outer space on Planet Zinfandel, and play with ideas all day. But now, as a politician in a country that opposed the war, I'll admit I screwed up, because politicians must deign to harness the wild mares of whimsy to the oxcart of cold, calculated reality." So, although his judgments were objectively wrong, they were contextually appropriate. Sweet! You've been totally 0wn3d by Michael Ignatieff! And so have all those dead Iraqis.

Immediately, I could tell: THIS ESSAY WASN'T GOING TO BE FRUSTRATING AT ALL.

Politicians cannot afford to cocoon themselves in the inner world of their own imaginings . . .

Why do I hear Geddy Lee singing this phrase over a 6/13 time signature? All that's missing is the phrase "telescopic counterfactuals / whispering nodes in my astronomy" and you've got a killer Rush lyric!

As a former denizen of Harvard, I've had to learn that a sense of reality doesn't always flourish in elite institutions. It is the street virtue par excellence. Bus drivers can display a shrewder grasp of what's what than Nobel Prize winners . . .

Given the title of my previous essay about Ignatieff, I was especially taken with this paragraph. Two questions:

1. Is Michael Ignatieff sending me secret messages, like Christopher Hitchens did Paul Wolfowitz? If so, let me state for the record: Michael Ignatieff, I am ready to wage war on whomever you want! You had me at "invade."

2. Don't bus drivers ever get tired of the "regular schmoes are smarter than us academics/politicians/ journalists" gag? Raise your hand if you think Ignatieff appointed any bus drivers to the Kennedy School faculty. I mean, if Ignatieff really thinks bus drivers are shrewder than academics, why didn't he quit Harvard and go drive a bus? After all, even if he turned out to be the worst bus driver ever, and ran over pedestrians every five seconds, he probably wouldn't kill as many people as his Iraq war did! (Joke.)

A sense of reality is not just a sense of the world as it is, but as it might be. Like great artists, great politicians see possibilities others cannot and then seek to turn them into realities . . .

Winston Churchill is Leonardo da Vinci. George W. Bush is Thomas Kinkade. Michael Ignatieff basically helped us buy a half-trillion dollars' worth of Thomas Kinkade paintings. Thanks.

To bring the new into being, a politician needs a sense of timing, of when to leap and when to remain still . . .

Come, now: if you're gonna steal from Kenny Rogers, you at least gotta grow the beard.

Few of us hear the horses coming . . .

"Ma! Circle the wagons! The horses are coming!" *"But Pa, I can't circle the wagons without the horses! The horses pull the wagons!"* "Oh, no! We're totally gonna get trampled by horses!"

Seriously, let's repeat this quote: "*Few of us hear the horses coming.*" We're really getting into Cormac McCarthy territory here . . .

They saw the WMDs over the hill, staggering under the weight of their own nonexistence like some funereal assemblage of bent-backed phantoms. Ignatieff crouched in the mulberry copse, glassed his target, cursed the Chomskian dust that risked his weapons ruin, then raised The Ultimate Task of Thomas Jeffersons Dream and sent its buckshot tearing into Iraq—tatterdemalion, sanction-wracked—and the rocks behind were splatter-stained with a crimson decoupage like some chromatic inversion of all that is holy and lawful. I kindly reckon we just shot the shit out of Iraq, Ignatieff said. And Friedman said, Lets move in to get a better look at her. And they tried hailing a cab with an anecdotaholic driver but they couldnt find one because they were stranded in a featureless semantic apocalypse, meaning-raped and apostropheless like some joy-smudged, italicized parody of Cormac McCarthy. And on the crest of the hill they heard Kanan Makiya weeping soundlessly like the very enabler of evil itself.

• • •

People do want leadership, and even when a leader is nonplussed by events, he must still remember to give the people the reassurance they deserve. Part of good judgment consists of knowing when to keep up appearances . . .

I think it was at about this point I started weeping quietly. "When will this essay end," I remember thinking, "and what will be left of my dignity? Is there a leader out there, steadfast and un-nonplussed, who can give me the reassurance I deserve?"

Improvisation may not stave off failure. The game usually ends in tears . . .

You know what would have pushed this essay into the realm of literary greatness? If Ignatieff had ended this paragraph with: "The game usually ends in tears—the tears of a clown." I don't know why, but that would have made me really happy. I guess because I love that song? Do you think there's a chance Ignatieff actually *did* consider ending with "the tears of a clown," but then deleted it, saying, "They wouldn't understand . . . they're not ready yet"? Let's call the Geek Squad and pay them to steal his hard drive! Then we can hacker-jack it.

The sign on Truman's desk—'The buck stops here!'—reminds us that those who make good judgments in politics tend to be those who do not shrink from the responsibility of making them . . .

Bingo! Our first tautology. You spend enough time in the vague-o-sphere, you're bound to bump into one.

Politicians have to learn to appear invulnerable without appearing inhuman. Being human, they are bound to revenge insults. But they also have to learn that revenge, as it has been said, is a dish best served cold . . .

My eyes. Stinging. Is it tears, or blood? Can't tell—all the mirrors are cracked. From my screams.

Nothing is personal in politics, because politics is theater. It is part of the job to pretend to have emotions that you do not actually feel. . . . This saving hypocrisy of public life is not available in private life. There we play for keeps . . .

I panicked when I read this, because I couldn't figure out where "we play for keeps": in private life, or in public life? I don't care if we play for keeps in public life—I never leave my house, so I don't *have* a public life. But if we play for keeps in private life, I'm doomed. Because I spend 90% of my waking hours in private. On the internet. And I don't want that to be "for keeps." Believe me, that must not be "for keeps."

> *Good judgment means understanding how to be responsible to those who pay the price of your decisions. . . . Sometimes sacrificing my judgment to [my constituents'] is the essence of my job. Provided, of course, that I don't sacrifice my principles . . .*

Attention, Michael Ignatieff's constituents: HE THINKS YOU'RE DUMB. Also, there's something suspicious about that "Provided, of course . . ." It's only five syllables, but it seems to mask a conga line of condescension. It makes me think Ignatieff assumes his *readers* are dumb, too. But I'm not dumb—I predicted the Iraq war would be a disaster. And that means I'm as smart as a bus driver.

> *Politicians with good judgment bend the policy to fit the human timber . . .*

Who was that poet who lived in the woods back in Civil War days? Ralph Waldo Emerson? Walt Whitman? Anyway, I'm sure he talked like this all the time: "I ain't payin' your confounded taxes—they don't fit my human timber! Because ye didn't bend 'em correctly! By the way, you're standin' on my sarsaparilla patch! Did they invent electricity yet?"

> *Resisting the popular isn't easy, because resisting the popular isn't always wise . . .*

Michael Ignatieff is the Chuck Klosterman of political science.

> *(Bush) had led a charmed life, and in charmed lives warning bells do not sound . . . . People with good judgment listen to warning bells within . . .*

Ding-dong! There's my warning bell within! What are you say-ing, warning bell? *Ding-dong! Don't keep reading this essay! Your HMO won't cover the neurological damage! Ding-aling-dong!*

> *A prudent leader will save democracies from the worst, but prudent leaders will not inspire a democracy to give its best . . .*

This reminds me of something I had stitched on the back of my denim jacket once: "An eagle with a broken wing may fly high enough to avoid the quicksand, but it cannot soar above possibility's treetops at the dawn of a new day." Boy, did everyone in town hate that denim jacket!

> *Daring leaders can be trusted as long as they give some inkling of knowing what it is to fail. They must be men of sorrow acquainted with grief, as the prophet Isaiah says . . .*

I think it's reaching to call Isiah Thomas a "prophet," though the New York Knicks are definitely "men of sorrow acquainted with grief." Surely Ignatieff doesn't think America would be better off if the New York Knicks were president? How would that even work? Also, he misspelled "Isiah."

In conclusion, this part of Ignatieff's essay should have been called "All I Really Need to Know I Learned in Kindergarten—But It Didn't Actually Sink in Until Thousands and Thousands of Iraqis Went to Heaven."

•••

Now, let's move on to the other part of the essay! Are you still with me? I still have some water in my canteen; I'll share it with you. No, don't be silly, there's plenty of light left—sunset's at least an hour away . . .

Next is the part of Ignatieff's essay that I initially thought would be the whole essay: the part where Ignatieff admits he made a boo-boo.

We might test judgment by asking, on the issue of Iraq, who best anticipated how events turned out. But many of those who correctly anticipated catastrophe did so not by exercising judgment but by indulging in ideology. They opposed the invasion because they believed the president was only after the oil or because they believed America is always and in every situation wrong.

"Always and in every situation wrong?" Come on, we all like it when America wins at the Olympics, right? I bet even Ward Churchill had a crush on Mary Lou Retton, back in the day. Good thing they didn't make a baby together, though! Wow! That would have been an intense baby—unlimited negative energy vs. unlimited positive energy and all that! For real, though: You anti-war people have got to admit, Ignatieff has you nailed. You dumb-asses who were right about everything for the wrong reasons, instead of wrong about everything for the right reasons. You lose.

The people who truly showed good judgment on Iraq predicted the consequences that actually ensued but also rightly evaluated the motives that led to the action. They did not necessarily possess more knowledge than the rest of us. They labored, as everyone did, with the same faulty intelligence and lack of knowledge of Iraq's fissured sectarian history. What they didn't do was take wishes for reality. They didn't suppose, as President Bush did, that because they believed in the integrity of their own motives everyone else in the region would believe in it, too. They didn't suppose that a free state could arise on the foundations of 35 years of police terror. They didn't suppose that America had the power to shape political outcomes in a faraway country of which most Americans knew little. They didn't believe that because

America defended human rights and freedom in Bosnia and Kosovo it had to be doing so in Iraq. They avoided all these mistakes.

Yeah, you're right, they did. Do you know why? *Because they're not retarded.*

I made some of these mistakes and then a few of my own. The lesson I draw for the future is to be less influenced by the passions of people I admire—Iraqi exiles, for example—and to be less swayed by my emotions . . .

And here, finally, is where my skull cracked open, my heart combusted, and a murder of crows flew out of my ass. Michael Ignatieff is drawing lessons for the future. Michael Ignatieff has a future in public policy. Sure, it's CANADIAN public policy, so it doesn't really count, but still—it's like the guy can't be stopped. You know why? Because he's at that level where you literally can't make a big enough mistake to be fired, shunned, or indicted. I'd like to visit that level someday. First thing I'd do is get rip-roarin' drunk and rob a bank using Richard Perle's face as a weapon. (JOKE!)

Then again, I guess it's for the best—because if people like Michael Ignatieff were ignored, how would we know what to think about the world?

Oh, wait: We could ask the bus drivers.

But now that I think about it, why ask bus drivers when we could ask RACE CAR DRIVERS? Race car drivers are smarter than bus drivers, right? After all, they make more money, are held in higher esteem, and have sexier wives!

RACE CAR DRIVERS ARE #1!

THE END.

Farewell, you incredible shithead.

August 14, 2007

Panel 1: How can Karl Rove quit the White House? He hasn't built his permanent Republican majority yet!

Panel 2: Oh, shit, you're right! How will America survive the twenty-first century without a permanent Republican majority?

Panel 3: The same way a baby survives without a steel-toe boot kicking her in the face every seven seconds?

August 14, 2007*

Panel 4: Remember when everyone thought Karl Rove was a genius, and that Republicans would never lose another election?

Panel 5: Even I thought he was a genius. An evil genius, sure, but a genius nonetheless.

Panel 6: I hope everybody learned their lesson: *Just because some asshole has a forehead the size of a watermelon and no conscience, doesn't mean he's a genius.*

August 14, 2007

"Americans earned a smaller average income in 2005 than in 2000, the fifth consecutive year that they had to **MAKE ENDS MEET WITH LESS MONEY** than at the peak of the last economic expansion." (*The New York Times*, 8/21/07)

Don't worry, a new economic expansion is right around the corner.

How can you be so sure?

Because the tax cuts on capital gains and dividends will deflate the stock market for ordinary Americans, making the tides rise. . . so the boats go higher. . . the boats have groceries on them, and you trade the groceries for gas. . . It's called "trickle down!"

Wow! *You don't even know what's supposed to trickle.*

August 21, 2007

I CAN HAS CHEEZBURGER?

August 27, 2007

Well, the partisan witch hunters finally got rid of Alberto Gonzales.

Oh, come on! That's an insult to the fine art of witch hunting. A witch hunt is *hard work*. It should be ingenious, nefarious. Making Gonzales look bad wasn't the result of a witch hunt—it was the result of *placing a microphone in the proximity of his mouth.*

So, you admit: If we lived in a land with no microphones and no electricity, Gonzales would still be attorney general!

August 28, 2007

*August 28, 2007**

September 3, 2007

September 3, 2007

I love playing in my hard-rock band! It's like a dream come true. There's only one problem. . .

Sometimes after a long rehearsal, my arms get stuck in *"jammin' key-boarder"* position.

. . . So I walk around looking like a zombie.

September 3, 2007

Do Iraqis know we're blaming them for everything that's gone wrong over there?

Well, SHOULDN'T we blame them? After all, whose country did we invade?

Actually, can I change the subject? I just had a crushing, depressing intuition that Hillary Clinton is gonna be our next president. That makes me really frustra—*Dude, stop laughing!* I'm not trying to be funny!

September 3, 2007

"For me, every day is an anniversary of September 11. . ." —Rudy Giuliani, 9/7/07

It must be hard to celebrate the anniversary of 9/11 *every single day.* I bet even Osama bin Laden doesn't do *that.*

I think it means Giuliani spends every day running around in a panic, wondering, *"Do people think I look like Winston Churchill yet?"*

I guess a benefit of every day being 9/11 is that you only need one page in your day planner.

September 11, 2007*

September 11, 2007

September 11, 2007

September 18, 2007

Iraqi Crybaby Theatre

Boo-hoo! The Americans want permanent military bases in my country!

I guess I should be happy—it means I'll always have someone to blame for my own problems!

But . . . but . . . that means the Americans have actually *selflessly helped me again!* Waah!

September 17, 2007

When I heard Hillary threatened to deny *GQ* access to Bill if they ran a story about her campaign, I thought, "Is she too chickenshit to be president?"

But she condemned the Iranian president's proposed visit to Ground Zero—that took real courage.

Great. Maybe she can be the Rudy Giuliani for people who hate male-pattern baldness.

September 24, 2007

Who would've thought we'd see an accusation of too much deadly force coming from a firm called "Blackwater?" The fuckin' name only sounds like an evil wizard's military compound.

Why not just call themselves *"Deathfang's Midnight Posse of Merciless Skull Warriors?"*

Well, the mercenaries would get erections every time they announced them-selves, for one thing.

September 24, 2007

Thank God we kept Mahmoud Ahmadinejad from visiting Ground Zero. That's sacred ground.

Is there a way to keep Ahmadinejad from even *thinking* about Ground Zero?

Probably. If there's one thing we've learned, it's easy to keep people from thinking when Ground Zero is involved.

September 24, 2007

Remember when we first started *Operation: Enduring Freedom?* Did you ever think it'd be so enduring — and *endearing?*

Sigh. Now *that* was a huge, expensive, open-ended military campaign I could get behind! I miss those days.

I used to have a friend who was skeptical about whether bombing the shit out of people was the best way to fight terrorism. *I bet he feels pretty stupid right now.*

October 8, 2007

"Iraqi leaders argue that sectarian animosity is **ENTRENCHED IN THE STRUCTURE OF THEIR GOVERNMENT.** Instead of reconciliation, they now stress alternative and perhaps more attainable goals. . ." —*The Washington Post*, 10/8/07

I can't wait to hear what the new, "*more attainable goals*" for Iraq will be.

One of the attainable goals could be, "Make a list of all the goals that are no longer attainable."

Nope: Making a list of all the goals that are no longer attainable in Iraq would take so goddamn long, *making the list itself* would have to be added to the list.

October 8, 2007

October 8, 2007

October 9, 2007

October 15, 2007

"As the Bush administration deals with the fallout from the recent **KILLINGS OF CIVILIANS** by private security firms in Iraq, some officials are asking whether the contractors could be considered **UNLAWFUL COMBATANTS** under international agreements." — *The Los Angeles Times*, 10/15/07

Can an irony be "delicious" even if it makes you sick?

Does this mean the Blackwater dudes will be shipped off to Guantanamo?

As long as the U.S. government is hiring unlawful combatants, why not use al-Qaeda? I hear those guys are *deadly*.

October 15, 2007

I'm starting to get the feeling that America has jumped the shark — that invading Iraq was the beginning of the end for us.

For some reason, the subprime-mortgage crisis is the news event that makes me think our run is over.

Um, guys? You should have wised up when they made a sequel to *The Cannonball Run*. That was TWENTY-THREE YEARS AGO.

October 22, 2007

We gotta do something about Iran! NOW! *They're the biggest threat we face!!!*

Oh, get over yourself. Iran's military expenditures are *less than one percent* of ours. You really think they're gonna attack us?

HOW *DARE* YOU NOT VALIDATE MY FEELINGS?!?

October 22, 2007

Panel 1: Now we got *Turkey* meddling in Iraq, along with Syria and Iran? Is anyone *not* totally meddling their ass off in Iraq?

Panel 2: What do you expect? We led by example. We've been some meddlesome motherfuckers, you must admit.

Panel 3: No, sorry— we're paying HALF A TRILLION DOLLARS to screw around in Iraq. We've earned a better verb than "meddle." We deserve a synonym with like, 125,000 syllables.

October 22, 2007

Panel 4: How much weaker is the dollar gonna get? Does it make financial sense to start using 'em as coffee filters yet?

Panel 5: Don't be ridiculous! The American dollar is still the world's favorite currency. It represents: STRENGTH and MUSCLES.

Panel 6: Yeah, I gotta admit, the dollar's still looking pretty strong—against the fuckin' *nickel*. And it continues to trade *much* higher than the penny.

Panel 7: They should change the name of the dollar to "The Penny Clobberer!"

October 29, 2007

Panel 8: Why are the Democrats still rolling over for Bush? The guy's approval rating looks like the calorie count for a lite beer!

Panel 9: Yeah, but remember: All it would take is another terror attack, and Bush's approval rating would jump back up to the 90's and he'd turn into Winston Churchill again. Democrats can't risk opposing that hypothetical Churchill.

Panel 10: I'd love to see a wrestling match between Bush's inner Churchill and Giuliani's inner Churchill—two dumb-ass historical analogies in matching unitards, beating the crap out of each other. Everybody wins!

November 5, 2007

Why can't people admit waterboarding is torture? The Khmer Rouge used it— isn't that good enough?

The Khmer Rouge also ate rice. *Does that mean eating rice is torture?* BOOM! I just totally won this argument! And by the way, what if there was a ticking nuclear bomb and we captured the only man who knew the combination to turn it off, and we had to waterboard him to save billions of lives—*maybe even trillions of lives?* Ha! Still think waterboarding is torture?

It must be, because all of a sudden I want to waterboard *you.*

November 5, 2007*

Pat Robertson has endorsed Giuliani! I love it!

But Rudy Giuliani is pro-choice and hangs out with gay people!

Totally! And I'm sure Robertson's gonna give him hell about that— *JUST AS SOON AS GIULIANI KILLS THE LAST MUSLIM ON EARTH.*

November 12, 2007

Do you worry about the future?

You mean, like, killer androids and stuff?

No, I don't mean like "*outer-space-robot-battles future.*" I mean just the regular ol' future. Of America. Do you think the country will be doing well in, say, forty years?

HA!!!

I know, right?!?

November 12, 2007

 I think the subprime mortgage crisis is the *most abstract thing* that has ever given me the creeps.

 I know. I hear people fretting about "collateralized debt obligations" and "structured investment vehicles" and I'm like, "Whatever! Just tell me when it's OK to kill all the millionaires."

 But if you murder all the rich people, who will remind you how exciting capitalism is?

November 12, 2007

 My sister doesn't have health insurance, so she doesn't see a doctor regularly.

 Now she's running a fever and feels a weird pressure in her abdomen. I'm scared for her. . . . I'm scared she'll start supporting *socialized medicine.*

 *Don't say that!* Your sister's gotta stay strong! Remind her: *BETTER DEAD THAN RED.*

November 16, 2007

 You know, between Vladimir Putin and Pervez Musharraf, I'm starting to think maybe President Bush isn't the best judge of character.

 You think Bush's *soul-looking-into* and *gut-feeling-following* abilities aren't as great as we all thought?

 Yeah. I'm at the point where if Bush even smiled at me, I'd have to assume I was a kleptomaniac or murderer or something.

November 19, 2007

November 26, 2007

November 26, 2007

"A White House assessment of the war in Afghanistan has concluded that **WIDE-RANGING STRATEGIC GOALS** that the Bush administration set for 2007 **HAVE NOT BEEN MET**. . ." — *The Washington Post*, 11/25/07

November 26, 2007

December 3, 2007

December 3, 2007

December 3, 2007

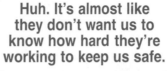

So the CIA deliberately destroyed recordings of "enhanced interrogation technique" sessions.

Huh. It's almost like they don't want us to know how hard they're working to keep us safe.

Maybe it isn't work to them.

December 10, 2007

Remember when we were all jazzed about President Bush's idea of an "Ownership Society?"

Heck yes! Get the government out of the way! Empower people to own their own stuff! Own your own home! Own your own health insurance!

Yeah, well, I'm over that. This whole mortgage crisis/credit crunch/looming recession has me jonesing for some *big-ass* government. They won't be able to *make* a government big-ass enough to satisfy me now.

December 17, 2007

Wouldn't it be cool if Mike Huckabee was president? Then America's nickname could be "*Huckabee Nation.*" I've always wanted to live in a country that sounds like a childrens' morning show!

I bet it'd be the first presidential inauguration to feature a jug band and a sarsaparilla-drinkin' contest.

It'd also be the first presidential inauguration to feature me throwing myself off a bridge. . .

December 17, 2007

December 23, 2007

December 28, 2007

December 28, 2007

NOOOO!!! Don't tell me Fred Thompson won't win the Republican nomination! He radiates the youthful, fresh-faced optimism America *needs* right now!

You must be joking— you could store *broccoli* in the bags under that dude's eyes.

I gotta say, I love how much the GOP establishment hates their candidates. Democrats should rent 'em Joe Biden, just to be sporting.

January 3, 2008

Did John McCain really say that if U.S. casualties dropped, Americans wouldn't care if we stayed in Iraq for *10,000 years*?

Yes, and it makes perfect sense—if you believe we invaded Iraq to minimize the casualties due to us invading Iraq.

You know, the best thing about McCain's scenario is, Iraq would get *10,000 years better.*

January 7, 2008

"Dampening the administration's **CUSTOMARY UPBEAT TONE** on the economy, President Bush acknowledged Monday that the economic signs were '**INCREASINGLY MIXED**'. . ."—The *New York Times*, 1/7/08

"Increasingly mixed"? Is that pseudo-Texan for *"impossibly fucked"?*

It's like saying the *Titanic* became *"increasingly moist"* after hitting the iceberg— like a couple good sponges could have solved the problem.

Wow, a *Titanic* analogy? You must be one of those bold, paradigm-shifting visionaries God sometimes sends to save our economy.

January 7, 2008

Do you have high hopes for Bush's trip to the Middle East this week?

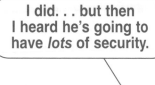

I did. . . but then I heard he's going to have *lots* of security.

You know, you really shouldn't joke about that.

January 7, 2008

I hope Hillary wins the Democratic nomination. It'll be fun to see her and Bill put the White House furniture back the way *they* like it.

Are you out of your mind? You're okay with the keys to the White House being passed back and forth between Bushes and Clintons like it's a goddamn *Myrtle Beach time-share*?

Hey, it beats getting my hopes up. . .

January 14, 2008

I heard Bush told Ehud Olmert that the National Intelligence Estimate "doesn't reflect his views on Iran."

That's understandable. After all, while the NIE is the consensus view of all sixteen intelligence agencies, it doesn't bother to include the views of non-real, hypothetical intelligence agencies that exist only in the President's mind.

WHY NOT?!? Those agencies are probably a lot more exciting!

January 14, 2008

Panel 1:

I don't understand Bill Clinton's anger towards Obama.

Panel 2:

Dude, Obama's messin' with the LEGACY! There was a plan! *NONE SHALL THWART THE DYNASTY!!!*

Panel 3:

Good ol' baby boomers. They act all love-dovey—until someone suggests they're not the center of the universe.

January 21, 2008

"The *New York Times* found 121 cases in which veterans of Iraq and Afghanistan **COMMITTED A KILLING** in this country, or were charged with one, after their **RETURN FROM WAR**. . ."—The *New York Times*, 1/20/08

Panel 1:

So now our veterans are coming home and *murdering innocent people?* Did the Army forget to design an "off" switch?

Panel 2:

I think any soldier who's due to come home but still feels a little bloodlust should stay in Iraq a bit longer, to work it out of their system.

Panel 3:

Seriously! It's like they've gone crazy—they think American lives are worth as little as *off-brand lives.*

January 21, 2008

Panel 1:

I love how Mitt Romney always brags about how he organized the Olympics! That's, like, two steps up from running a water park.

Panel 2:

Ooh! Ooh! I was a shift manager at Disney World! Can I be president?

Panel 3:

What's so hard about it? Just build a pole-vaulting vault, rent a big-ass pool, round up some pommel horses, book a bunch of hotel rooms, and make sure you've got enough medals! DONE. And you've got *four fucking years* to do it!

January 21, 2008

Who do you think would win the election, if it was between Hillary and McCain?

Ugh. Can we *please* talk about something less depressing?

How about: We're entering a global recession and you're going to die broke and hungry.

Now we're getting somewhere!

January 21, 2008

One thing I respect about Hillary: She worked with Republicans to sponsor legislation that would have made flag-burning illegal.

Why does that make you respect her?

It proves she can reach across the aisle to achieve meaningless bullshit!

January 28, 2008

I watched a Giuliani stump speech on C-Span last night. Did you know one of his campaign promises is to fly to Mars?

Wait—you mean *Giuliani himself* is gonna fly to Mars? Shit, I'd vote to see that.

Ha! Like it would be possible for Giuliani to exist on a planet that hadn't experienced 9/11.

January 28, 2008

February 4, 2008

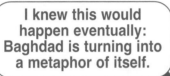

"**BAGHDAD IS DROWNING IN SEWAGE,** thirsty for water and largely powerless, an Iraqi official said on Sunday in a grim assessment of services in the capital five years after the US-led invasion."—Agence France-Presse, 2/3/08

February 4, 2008

February 4, 2008

Panel 1 (February 12, 2008):

What do you think about all these teenagers and college kids Obama's bringing to his rallies?

I don't like it! If young people get all fired up about *politics*, it might sap their energy—valuable energy that could be used in Iraq!

Exactly! They'll have plenty of time to vote when they're older. Y'know, if they. . . *last.*

February 12, 2008

Panel 2 (February 12, 2008):

"(Democrats) say, '*Oh, we're only going to tax the rich people*,' but most people in America understand that the rich people hire good accountants and figure out how not to necessarily pay all the taxes. . ."—President Bush, 2/10/08

I gotta say, Bush sounds pretty defeatist about the situation. Where's his famous fightin' spirit?

Would it be easier if we just repealed *all* taxes on rich people?

No, that would put too many amoral accountants out of work. We need a federal program that *subsidizes tax-avoidance accountants for middle-class and poor people.* Unfair is unfair!

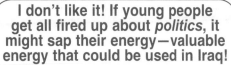

February 12, 2008

Panel 3 (February 18, 2008):

"A suicide car bomber killed 38 Afghans at a crowded market Monday, pushing the death toll from **TWO DAYS OF MILITANT BOMBINGS** to about 140."—The *Washington Post*, 2/18/08

The deteriorating situation in Afghanistan raises an interesting question: *How many wars can we lose at the same time?*

Don't be a defeatist! We'll win in Afghanistan just as soon as someone takes the time to figure out what "winning" is. The only reason nobody's done that yet is that we're *too busy winning.*

But after six years of non-stop winning, shouldn't we be closer to having won?

February 18, 2008

"Fidel Castro announced early Tuesday morning that he is stepping down as Cuba's president, **ENDING HIS HALF-CENTURY RULE** of the island nation."—The *Washington Post*, 2/19/08

Another tyrant has fallen! See? Embargoes work! Refusing to meet with dictators gets *results*! You just have to be patient. . .

Great. Remind me to buy you a beer when Ahmadinejad steps down in 46 years.

Oh, I will *so* be ready to drink that beer! And by the way, it's gonna be a Michelob Ultra, and it's gonna taste *ultra delicious*.

February 18, 2008

So Musharraf got his ass kicked in the Pakistani elections. Is now when I panic about the Googly-Eyed Bearded Ones taking over the country?

What if that didn't happen? What if Pakistan became kind of stable and boring?

God, then I'd be *so* tempted to invade it.

February 18, 2008

How bad do you think the recession is gonna be? Will I have to trade my house for grain and move into my car?

It's gonna be uglier than Sylvester Stallone's falsetto. If food and fuel prices keep going up, I expect to see fart-filled paper bags being traded on the commodities market. I'm getting a tattoo of honey mustard on my arm, *in case I ever have to eat it.*

Hell, if food prices keep going up, I may finally have to eat this doughnut!

February 26, 2008

If John McCain is our next president, will we invade more countries?

Shit, honey—he'll probably invade a country just to celebrate winning the election.

Someone should really tell him there's no shame in taking Viagra.

February 26, 2008

"For the first time in U.S. history, **MORE THAN ONE OF EVERY 100 ADULTS IS IN JAIL OR PRISON,** according to a new report documenting America's rank as the world's No. 1 incarcerator."—The Associated Press, 2/28/08

We finally broke the one-percent mark! Nothing can stop us! (If we don't all wind up in prison, of course.)

All those people fretting about China's growth—"*Ooh, we can't compete with China's numbers!*" Well, guess what? *Yes. We. Can.* Eat it, China! Have fun letting more than 99% of your adult population run around all free and un-jailed, you losers.

I wish I owned stock in prisons. Then I wouldn't worry about recessions.

February 29, 2008

Do you think phone companies should illegally spy on us if the White House asks them to?

If the White House asks them to, how can it be "illegal?" Also, if the one-eyed man is king, how can he be blind — *or play the banjo???*

God, I hope the NSA is listening to your phone calls. It would serve 'em right.

February 29, 2008

February 29, 2008

March 10, 2008

March 10, 2008

Panel 1 (top left): Y'know, everyone talks about how inspirational it is to have a black guy and a woman running for president. . . what about a 71-year-old man?

Panel 2 (top middle): I agree McCain's candidacy is inspiring. It means that someday, I'll be able to kneel down and pat my loved one on the head and say, "Y'know, maybe in a few years *you* can run for president. . .

Panel 3 (top right): . . . Grandpa."

March 24, 2008

Panel 4 (middle left): So John McCain thinks Iran is training al-Qaeda. I know he's a maverick and all, but shouldn't he understand the difference between Sunnis and Shiites?

Panel 5 (middle middle): Give him a break! He's OLD. I wouldn't expect *my* grandfather to understand fuckin' *Biggie versus Tupac*, let alone all that complicated Sunni/Shiite shit. Hell, McCain probably gets *freaked out by digital clocks*. We should leave him be!

Panel 6 (middle right): Should we leave him be before or *after* we elect him president?

March 24, 2008

Panel 7 (bottom left): I noticed that the 4,000th American soldier was killed just a few days after the five-year anniversary of the Iraq war.

Panel 8 (bottom middle): It's creepy, right? Like watching your odometer turn over just as you pull into your driveway. Or something.

Panel 9 (bottom right): I almost wish the White House did it deliberately, to be poignant. At least then I'd know they were capable of *achieving something on purpose* over there.

March 24, 2008

I finally figured out how we can win in Iraq: Just carpet-bomb the country with unsold McMansions! Hell, we can probably sell 'em to the Pentagon by the pound.

NICE! I *knew* there had to be a silver lining to the imminent, catastrophic, devastating economic meltdown.

Say, now that I've proposed a dumb-ass idea that shows zero understanding of the Iraq War *or* the economy, will journalists start calling me a maverick and let me use their mouths as a dick-warmer?

March 25, 2008

So we're supporting the Islamic Supreme Council of Iraq—which was founded in *Iran*—as they battle Sadr's Mahdi army, which was *trained* by Iran?

No, Iran trained the ISCI's Badr brigades, *not* Sadr's Mahdi army. It's all a big power play over Basra. The Badr brigades—

Look: Are we fucking winning, or not?

March 31, 2008

Are you loving the tagline for John McCain's new ad? *"The American president Americans have been waiting for."*

Don't make fun—most of McCain's base probably has trouble remembering to take their Metamucil, let alone what country they live in.

You know what? Seriously? I *am* kind of sick of old people. Am I allowed to say that?

March 31, 2008

"Iraqi security forces are waging a tough battle against **MILITIA FIGHTERS AND CRIMINALS** in Basra—many of whom have received **ARMS AND TRAINING AND FUNDING FROM IRAN**. . ."—President Bush, 3/27/08

But wasn't it the *Badr brigades* who were trained by Iran? And aren't we *backing* the Badr brigades on behalf of Maliki?

Who's "Maliki?" One of those girl singers on the MTV with no clothes?

God, I can't wait until we elect John McCain and he can just *solve all this* with his integrity!

March 31, 2008

"Congress must not choose to lose in Iraq; we should choose instead to succeed."—John McCain, 4/8/08

Can we choose to travel backwards through time and then choose not to invade?

Sorry, that choice is not on the menu. Please choose from the available options: *Lose* or *Succeed*.

Hmm. . . Which choice is better? How do I decide? Hmm. Tough call. Aw, hell, fuck it: *Let's choose to SUCCEED!!!*

April 8, 2008

Why does John McCain keep saying al-Qaeda is Shiite? That's like saying Santa Claus is Jewish.

Oh, don't mind John McCain! Let him sit on his porch and yell at the whippersnappers. It's not like the poor guy will ever be in charge of anything, or make decisions that could lead to massive casualties or a nuclear war.

Umm. . .

If McCain *does* become president and launches a nuclear war, I call dibs on hiding in the folds in his neck!

April 15, 2008

How about this: Every time McCain says al-Qaeda is Shiite, you take a drink.

I like that, because by the time he's sworn in as our next president, I'll be dead from liver failure.

Say, are they going to swear him in on a large-print Bible?

April 15, 2008

So those ex-generals you see on TV analyzing the Iraq war have been secretly getting their talking points from the Defense Department! Sweet!

You know what they say: "*Once* a grumpy, square-jawed orders-following automaton, *always* a grumpy, square-jawed orders-following automaton."

I wonder how they're able to keep their posture so straight while fully bent over?

April 21, 2008

I just learned that most of those "military analysts" you see on cable are actually coached by the Pentagon and take money from military contractors.

So cheerleading for the war helps them make money. God bless 'em. Why should Iraqis be the only ones who benefit from all this?

Yeah, why should Iraqis be the only ones who benefit so, so, so much from all this?

April 21, 2008

Well, the Pennsylvania primary certainly changed everything — not. Remind me again why we had to wait a month and a god-damn half for that?

It's like being horribly constipated, taking a laxative, *waiting six weeks for it to work* and then . . . burping.

Six weeks. If we'd had to wait any longer, most of Hillary's base would have died of old age!

April 22, 2008

"Even as American and Iraqi troops are fighting to establish control of the Sadr City section of (Baghdad), the Iraqi government's program to **RESTORE BASIC SERVICES LIKE ELECTRICITY, SEWAGE AND TRASH COLLECTION** is lagging, jeopardizing the effort to win over the area's wary residents."—The *New York Times*, 4/22/08

Can we agree that the great lesson of the Iraq war is YOU GOTTA PICK UP THE TRASH?

Exactly. It's like, the more someone is surrounded by garbage and sewage, the less grateful they are to us.

But that's Freedom Sewage! It was pooped out by a liberated people! You guys talk as if it smells *bad*.

April 22, 2008

"'I think (Obama) just wants to be president **BECAUSE HE'S BLACK**,' said Tim Hetrick, smoking a cigarette as he waited for a bus among the crumbling structures of downtown McKeesport (PA). A Democrat, he's thinking about **VOTING FOR McCAIN** in November."—The *Washington Post*, 4/22/08

God, why do you blacks always want to be president? It's *so* annoying!

You know us blacks, always wanting to be president just because we're black. It's like we think we're entitled to it (because of how god-damn black we are).

When I read that quote, I realized why our economy is totally doomed: *You can't train 19th-century-minded motherfuckers for 21st-century jobs.*

April 28, 2008

Strip 1 — April 28, 2008

Man: Remember a few months ago, when we were joking about how the Republicans couldn't settle on a nominee and their party was tearing itself apart?

Woman: Yeah. . . good times.

Man: Agreed. That was fun. Karma sucks *ass*, by the way.

April 28, 2008

Strip 2 — May 6, 2008

"The number of suicides among veterans of wars in Iraq and Afghanistan **MAY EXCEED THE COMBAT DEATH TOLL** because of inadequate mental health care." —Bloomberg, 5/5/08

You know, of all the people involved in the Iraq War, it's not actually the *soldiers* who I wish would kill themselves. . . .

Remember when Bush played dress-up and landed on the aircraft carrier? He should see that role through to the end.

This is why we're losing: When the enemy commits suicide, they're in the middle of a crowd. When our kids do it, they're totally alone.

May 6, 2008

Strip 3 — May 6, 2008

"The number of suicides among veterans of wars in Iraq and Afghanistan **MAY EXCEED THE COMBAT DEATH TOLL** because of inadequate mental health care . . ." —*Bloomberg*, 5/5/08

I love how military culture considers it a *weakness* to seek psychological counseling. I love that.

So you want an army made up of weepy, introspective emo kids? You think fuckin' *Fall Out Boy* could've invaded Iraq?

You're right. I just hope we have the discipline not to learn anything from this, or else I won't be able to get excited for the next war.

May 6, 2008

Panel 1: I wonder how many Iraqis have committed suicide?

Panel 2: You mean the kind of committing suicide where they strap bombs to their chest and scream about Allah?

Panel 3: No, I mean the kind of committing suicide where they're just really depressed and sad.

May 6, 2008

Panel 4: I just saw a CNN poll that gives Bush a 71% disapproval rating.

Panel 5: I saw a Washington Post poll that says 82% of Americans think the country's on the wrong track.

Panel 6: The fact that it's taken *this* long to see those kinds of poll numbers makes me think Americans are so dumb, I should probably start *approving* of Bush on principle.

May 12, 2008

Panel 7: The Taliban is still strong in some regions of Afghanistan, but we hardly ever hear about it.

Panel 8: It's because Iraq became a distraction. If we hadn't invaded, we could've kept our focus on Afghanistan.

Panel 9: Yeah, right! Blame Iraq! I'm sure Americans would've become *total Afghanistan experts*, always demanding more news about Afghanistan. Face it: Afghanistan is *boring*, and there's not a goddamn thing Iraq can do about it.

May 12, 2008

Did you hear that President Bush gave up golf out of respect for the troops?

Wouldn't it have been more respectful to just give up being president?

May 19, 2008

"The inspector general for the Defense Department said yesterday that the **PENTAGON CANNOT ACCOUNT** for almost $15 billion worth of goods and services . . . that were bought from contractors in the Iraq reconstruction effort."
—The *Washington Post*, 5/23/08

The Pentagon is all like, "Waah, we could keep track of the money if only everyone would stop shooting at us!"

I'm sorry, but if you can build a bunch of fuckin' *Pizza Huts* on military bases in Iraq, you can keep track of your money!

Hell, I wouldn't bother keeping track of the money, either. It's not like we're gonna run out.

May 26, 2008

I hear Joe Lieberman is gonna speak at John Hagee's *"we-need-to-defend-Israel-so-God-can-come-down-and-save-the-Christians"* summit.

Is John Hagee the fat guy with the Barca-lounger voice who said the Catholic church was a Great Whore and Hitler was helping fulfill God's prophecy? I find him kind of intriguing.

Isn't it interesting that guys who say stuff like that are either sitting in the dark end of a bar. . . or running huge, multi-million-dollar ministries?

May 26, 2008

Did you know Iraq is becoming one of the biggest buyers of American-made weapons?

Makes sense: They've personally seen all the good those weapons can do.

There's something weird about what you just said, but I can't put my finger on it.

June 2, 2008

"Our will is being tested, but we are resolute. We have a better way. **STAY STRONG! STAY THE COURSE! KILL THEM!** Be confident! Prevail! We are going to wipe them out! **WE ARE NOT BLINKING!**" —President Bush, 4/6/04 (according to Lt. Gen. Ricardo Sanchez)

***Stay strong! Be confident! Prevail!* Does President Bush base his military instructions on Nike marketing campaigns?**

I like *"We are not blinking!"* It sounds like Borat bragging about the quality of his contact lenses.

And, of course, you gotta give it up for good ol' *"KILL THEM!"*

June 2, 2008

"John McCain honed his national security message before Jewish-American leaders, charging on Monday that Senator Barack Obama's policies toward Iraq and Iran would **CREATE CHAOS** and endanger the United States and Israel." —*The New York Times*, 6/3/08

If McCain is so opposed to chaos, why did he support the Iraq War?

Maybe he forgot to change the water in his steam-powered chaos sensor.

Seriously, isn't John McCain's *entire foreign policy* based on creating chaos in the Middle East? Or is he no longer pledging to bomb anyone browner than the inside of a day-old apple?

June 9, 2008*

June 9, 2008

June 16, 2008

June 16, 2008

June 23, 2008

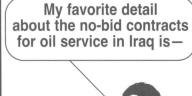

June 30, 2008

July 7, 2008

Do you think Bush will bomb Iran?

Not before November — the spike in gas prices would hurt Republicans more than the blood lust would help 'em. But I wouldn't be surprised if Bush bombs Iran as his last presidential act: *"I'll hand over the keys in a second, Barack; just gotta take care of one last thing. Now, where'd I leave that big red button?"*

Good ol' big red button! John McCain's been waiting to push it for so long, he probably drools on his lap when he sees a clown's nose.

July 14, 2008

I gotta say, everybody seems pretty chill about the fact that our government has tortured people.

Well, what are we *supposed* **to do? Organize some stupid march on Washington? Look, everyone knows it's kind of lame we're torturing people. But it's not the end of the world.**

See, that would be my attitude if we were only *metaphorically* **torturing people.**

July 21, 2008

I love this poll: You know how everyone says Obama isn't popular with Jewish voters? Turns out they like him more than they like Joe Lieberman!

That's the kind of poll result that warms my heart. I wish there was a way to literally *snuggle* **with that data.**

I know. I'm worried I'll get paper cuts on my tongue from making out with those bar graphs.

July 21, 2008

July 24, 2008

July 28, 2008

July 28, 2008

I'm sick of baby steps! Why can't Afghanistan defeat the Taliban, shut down its narco-economy, and get on its feet once and for all?

The Afghan government doesn't have the authority or strength to do shit. It isn't really a functioning country.

Oh really? Because when I look in my atlas, I see a weird blob-lookin' shape with a line all the way around it and the word "Afghanistan" typed in the middle. *Works for me!*

July 28, 2008

Would you mind if the White House forged documents to support the invasion of Iraq?

You mean, Would I mind if they forged them *now*? No, I'd think it was cute—especially if Bush forged them at a special Rose Garden ceremony, with all the media looking on respectfully.

None of it matters, does it?

Nope.

August 5. 2008

I just read that Afghanistan is now deadlier for our troops than Iraq. It's been seven years — why haven't we secured that place?

Let me ask you a question: What languages do Afghans speak?

How would I know? They probably speak *Islamo-muslim-inese* or *Goat-scratch-glish* or something. . . bunch of googly-eyed freaks. . .

Right. See you in another seven years!

August 7, 2008

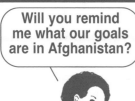
Will you remind me what our goals are in Afghanistan?

Same as Iraq: Large piles of dead terrorists. Freedom. Fewer beards. Bragging rights. Stability.

"Stability." How does that work, again?

Easy: You just invade a country and keep killing people until it calms down.

August 7, 2008

So after all the roundups and detainments and habeas-corpus-nots and pseudo-trials, the best we've got is one count against Osama bin Laden's fuckin' *chauffeur*? Maybe I'd be impressed—if somebody had tried to fly a fucking *limousine* into the World Trade Center.

Don't worry, it's just a first step. The bigger fish are yet to be fried.

Oh, fuck the fried fish. This is taking *forever*. Can we please shut down Guantanamo and get back to being a normal country?

Sure, just as soon as we've defeated all evil everywhere.

August 7, 2008

Remember the good ol' days of the anthrax scare? It was exhilarating, in a weird way.

I know what you mean—it was scary, but it was also so absurd, you couldn't take it seriously. It was like a novelty act of terror.

Though to be fair, *crashing airplanes into the World Trade Center towers and making them collapse* was novel as a MOTHERFUCKER.

That literally happened.

August 8, 2008

You know what's funny? I still don't actually know much about Iraq. Or Afghanistan. I mean, I know we're over there shooting guns and painting schools and spiriting people away to be tortured and whatnot, but I don't know what those places are *like*.

Why don't you ask someone who lives over there?

Are the people who are *still alive* really representative?

August 8, 2008

So Iraq is almost fixed; we'll withdraw by the end of 2010 or whenever. We can drop off a final load of food in Afghanistan on our way out of the region. Then everyone will come home. The End.

What happens if there's another terror attack?

Why would there be another terror attack?

August 8, 2008

As-Salaam Alaikum. Do you have any alcohol left in your cubicle? I've been studying current events again.

Shalom. There are five bottles of Jim Beam under my desk— two are empty and three are full. Come on over.

October 14, 2001

THANK YOU

Kassie Evashevski.

Richard Nash and Soft Skull Press.

Sean McDonald and Riverhead Books.

Lance Tilford. Craig Peskett.

David Jacobs, Nina Kang, and others who offered web site help.

Mike Houston and Martin Mazorra of Cannonball Press.

Amelia Kahaney, Erin Snider, Zach Hudson, and Nahela Hadi of Adopt-A-Minefield.

Eric Bates, Will Dana, and Jann Wenner of Rolling Stone.

The Rude Mechs Theatre Company.

Aaron Gray. John Hodgman. Bill Scher.

Norman Care (R.I.P.).

Matt Taibbi.

Mike Watt.

The men (and dogs) of Mine Detection and Dog Center Team #5.

My family and friends.

John Kearney, for that first conversation in the second week of October, 2001.

My parents.

My wife, Sarah.

MDC TEAM #5 FOR MOTHERFUCKIN' LIFE.